Table of Contents

Astrology Activated 2021:
Cutting Edge Insight Into the Ancient Art of Astrology
(Understanding Zodiac Signs and Horoscopes)

INTRODUCTION	3
HOW TO GET THE MOST OUT OF THIS BOOK	4
CHAPTER 1: THE CELESTIAL BODIES — THE PLANETS EXPLAINED	6
THE CREATION OF THE ZODIAC	6
HOW THE CELESTIAL BODIES AFFECT ASTROLOGY	7
The Sun	7
The Moon	8
Mars	9
Jupiter	9
Saturn	10
Mercury	10
Venus	11
Transcendental Planets	11
Uranus	12
Pluto	12
Neptune	13
THE ASTROLOGICAL WHEEL	13
CHAPTER 2: THE 12 SIGNS OF THE ZODIAC	16
ARIES (MARCH 21-APRIL 19) THE RAM	17
TAURUS (APRIL 20-MAY 21) THE BULL	18
GEMINI (MAY 21-JUNE 20) THE TWINS	20
CANCER (JUNE 21-JULY 22) THE CRAB	21
LEO (JULY 23-AUGUST 22) THE LION	22
VIRGO (AUGUST 23-SEPTEMBER 22) THE MAIDEN	24
LIBRA (SEPTEMBER 23-OCTOBER 22) THE SCALES	26
SCORPIO (OCTOBER 23-NOVEMBER 21) THE SCORPION	28
SAGITTARIUS (NOVEMBER 22-DECEMBER 21) THE ARCHER	29
CAPRICORN (DECEMBER 22-JANUARY 19) THE GOAT	30
AQUARIUS (JANUARY 20-FEBRUARY 18) THE WATER BEARER	31
PISCES (FEBRUARY 19-MARCH 20) THE FISH	33
CHAPTER 3: HOW TO READ YOUR NATAL CHART	36
HOW TO FIND YOUR SUN SIGN	36
WHAT THE HOUSES TELL US	37
Locating the Ascendant	38
The Astrological Houses Defined	38
HOW THE PLANETS PLAY A PART IN THE NATAL CHART	39
The First Set of Planets Are Personal Planets	39
The Second Set of Planets Are Outer Planets	40
UNDERSTANDING AND INTERPRETING YOUR CHART	40
CHAPTER 4: YOUR SUN SIGN AND YOU	43
SUN SIGNS IN ASTROLOGY AND THEIR MEANING	43

CHAPTER 5: HOW TO DETERMINE YOUR MOON SIGN 57

    Moon in Aries 58
    Moon in Taurus 58
    Moon in Gemini 58
    Moon in Cancer 59
    Moon in Leo 59
    Moon in Virgo 59
    Moon in Libra 60
    Moon and Scorpio 60
    Moon in Sagittarius 60
    Moon in Capricorn 61
    Moon in Aquarius 61
    Moon in Pisces 62

CHAPTER 6: YOUR RISING SIGN 64

    Aries Ascendant 64
    Taurus Ascendant 65
    Gemini Ascendant 66
    Cancer Ascendant 66
    Leo Ascendant 67
    Virgo Ascendant 68
    Libra Ascendant 68
    Scorpio Ascendant 69
    Sagittarius Ascendant 69
    Capricorn Ascendant 70
    Aquarius Ascendant 71
    Pisces Ascendant 72

CHAPTER 7: ARE YOU BORN ON A CUSP? 74

    Aries-Taurus Cusp (April 17–23) — The Cusp of Power 74
    Taurus-Gemini Cusp (May 17–23) — The Cusp of Energy 75
    Gemini-Cancer Cusp (June 18–24) — The Cusp of Magic 76
    Cancer-Leo Cusp (July 19–25) — The Cusp of Oscillation 77
    Leo-Virgo Cusp (August 19–25) — The Cusp of Exposure 78
    Virgo-Libra Cusp (September 19–25) — The Cusp of Beauty 79
    Libra-Scorpio Cusp (October 19–25) — The Cusp of Drama 80
    Scorpio-Sagittarius Cusp (November 18–24) — The Cusp of Revolution 81
    Sagittarius-Capricorn Cusp (December 28–24) — The Cusp of Prophecy 82
    Capricorn-Aquarius Cusp (January 17–23) — The Cusp of Mystery and Imagination 82
    Aquarius-Pisces Cusp (February 15–21) — The Cusp of Sensitivity 83
    Pisces-Aries Cusp (March 17–23) — The Cusp of Rebirth 84

CHAPTER 8: ARE YOU COMPATIBLE? 87

    Love Secrets of Venus 87
        Venus in Aries 88
        Venus in Taurus 89
        Venus in Gemini 90
        Venus in Cancer 91
        Venus in Leo 92
        Venus in Virgo 93
        Venus in Libra 94
        Venus in Scorpio 95

- *Venus in Sagittarius* 96
- *Venus in Capricorn* 97
- *Venus in Aquarius* 98
- *Venus in Pisces* 99

CHAPTER 9: HOW TO READ YOUR DAILY HOROSCOPE 100

- WHY DO PEOPLE READ THEIR HOROSCOPE? 100
- HOW ARE HOROSCOPES CREATED? 101
- THE CORRECT WAY TO READ YOUR HOROSCOPE 101
- WHAT ABOUT YOUR SUN SIGN? 102

CHAPTER 10: THE EFFECT OF ASTROLOGY ON DIFFERENT RELIGIONS AND CULTURES 103

- THE CHINESE ZODIAC 103
  - *Effects on Relationships* 103
  - *Religion* 104
  - *Other Countries Influenced by the Chinese Zodiac* 104
  - *Mythology — Racing to the Finish* 105
- HINDUISM ASTROLOGY 107
  - *The Principle of Vedic Astrology* 107
  - *The Predictive Vedic Astrology* 107

CONCLUSION 109

DESCRIPTION 110

NUMEROLOGY 2021:
Your Destiny Decoded: Personal Numerology For Beginners

INTRODUCTION 113

CHAPTER 1: WHAT IS NUMEROLOGY? 115

CHAPTER 2: THE PHILOSOPHY OF NUMBERS 118

- A LITTLE HISTORY 120
- PYTHAGORAS, FATHER OF NUMEROLOGY 125
- MISUNDERSTOOD NUMBERS 126

CHAPTER 3: HOW TO USE THIS BOOK 128

- USING CORRESPONDENTS 130
- COLORS, GEMS, CRYSTALS, AND VEGETATION 131
- FOOD 132
- MUSIC NOTES, APPEALS, AND INSTRUMENTS 134

CHAPTER 4: HOW TO FIND YOUR NUMBERS: CHALLENGE NUMBER 135

- INSIDE A CASK 136
- FIND THE NUMBERS: CHALLENGE 137
- INSTRUCTIONS FOR THE NUMBER TABLE: CHALLENGE 137
- NUMBER: CHALLENGE SYSTEM 138
- THE NUMBER TIME: CHALLENGE TIME 140
- CATEGORIES OF PERSONALITY 141
- BASIC RULES FOR NAME INTERPRETATION 141
- CATEGORIES OF PERSONALITY: PURPOSE AND INSTRUCTIONS 142
  - *Automation* 142
  - *Self-Image* 143
  - *Self-Expression* 143
- THE NUMBERS HAVE A POSITIVE SIDE AND A NEGATIVE SIDE 144

- Destination Number: Purpose and Instructions 146
- Instructions for Finding the Number of the Destination 147
- The Number of the Personal Year: Purpose and Instructions 148
  - *Personal Year Number 1* 149
  - *Personal Year Number 2* 149
  - *Personal Year Number 3* 149
  - *Personal Year Number 4* 149
  - *Personal Year Number 5* 149
  - *Personal Year Number 6* 150
  - *Personal Year Number 7* 150
  - *Personal Year Number 8* 150
  - *Personal Year Number 9* 150
- Instructions to Find Your Personal Year 150
  - *Method 1: Using Personal Year Quadriculates* 150
  - *Method 2: Using System Year* 151
- Numerical Comparisons 152

CHAPTER 5: NUMBER 1 – INDEPENDENCE 156

- Attributes 156
- Correspondents 156
- Challenges of the Number 1 157
- Physical Challenges of the Number 1 159
- Balancing the Challenges of the Number 1 161
- Automotive 161
- Self-Image 163
- Self-Expression 164
- Destiny 165
- Personal Year 165
- Personal Month 166
- Personal Day 166

CHAPTER 6: NUMBER 2 – COOPERATION 168

- Attributes 168
- Correspondents 168
- Challenges of the Number 2 169
- Physical Challenges of the Number 2 171
- Balancing the Challenges of the Number 2 173
- Automotive 173
- Self-Image 175
- Self-Expression 176
- Destiny: 177
- Personal Year 177
- Personal Month 178
- Personal Day 178

CHAPTER 7: NUMBER 3 – COMMUNICATION 179

- Attributes 179
- Correspondents 179
- Challenges of the Number 3 180
- Physical Challenges of the Number 3: 181
- Balancing the challenges of the Number 3 182
- Self-Image 182
- Self-Expression 183

- Destiny: 184
- Personal Year 184
- Personal Month 185
- Personal Day 186

CHAPTER 8: NUMBER 4 – PRACTICALITY 188

- Attributes 188
- Correspondents 188
- Challenges of the Number 4 189
- Physical Challenges of the Number 4 191
- Balancing the Challenges of the number 4 192
- Automotive 192
- Self-Image 194
- Self-Expression 195
- Destiny 196
- Personal Year 196
- Personal Month 197
- Personal Day 198

CHAPTER 9: NUMBER 5 – SEXUAL FREEDOM 199

- Attributes 199
- Correspondents 199
- Challenges of the Number 5 200
- Physical Challenges of the Number 5 202
- Balancing The Challenge Of Number 5 203
- Automotive 203
- Self-Image 205
- Self-Expression 206
- Destiny 207
- Personal Year 207
- Personal Month 208
- Personal Day 209
- Attributes 210
- Correspondents 210
- Challenges Of The Number 6 211
- Physical Challenges of the Number 6 213
- Balancing the Challenges of the Number 6 214
- Automotive 214
- Self-Image 216
- Self-Expression 217
- Destiny 218
- Personal Year 218
- Personal Month 219
- Personal Day 220

CHAPTER 11: NUMBER 7 – MENTAL ANALYSIS 221

- Attributes 221
- Correspondents 221
- Challenges of the Number 7 222
- Physical Challenges of the Number 7 225
- Balancing the Challenges of the Number 7 227
- Automotive 228
- Self-Image 232

- Self-Expression 234
- Destiny 237
- Personal Year 237
- Personal Month 239
- Personal Day 239

CHAPTER 12: NUMBER 8 – MATERIAL POWER 241

- Attributes 241
- Correspondents 241
- Challenges of the Number 8 242
- Physical Challenges of the Number 8 244
- Balancing the Challenges of the Number 8 245
- Automotive 246
- Self-Image 247
- Self-Expression 248
- Destiny: 250
- Personal Year 250
- Personal Month 251
- Personal Day 251

CHAPTER 13: NUMBER 9 AND 0 – CONCLUSIONS 253

- Attributes 254
- Correspondents 254
- The Challenges of the Numbers 9 and 0 255
- Physical Challenges of the Numbers 9 and 0 257
- Balancing the Challenges of the Numbers 9 and 0 258
- Automotive 258
- Self-Image 260
- Self-Expression 261
- Destiny 263
- Personal Year 263
- Personal Month 264
- Personal Day 265

CONCLUSION 267

Astrology Activated 2021:

Cutting Edge Insight Into the Ancient Art of Astrology (Understanding Zodiac Signs and Horoscopes)

By: Serra Night

☐ Copyright 2019 by Serra Night - All rights reserved.

This content is provided with the sole purpose of providing relevant information on a specific topic for which every reasonable effort has been made to ensure that it is both accurate and reasonable. Nevertheless, by purchasing this content you consent to the fact that the author, as well as the publisher, are in no way experts on the topics contained herein, regardless of any claims as such that may be made within. As such, any suggestions or recommendations that are made within are done so purely for entertainment value. It is recommended that you always consult a professional prior to undertaking any of the advice or techniques discussed within.

This is a legally binding declaration that is considered both valid and fair by both the Committee of Publishers Association and the American Bar Association and should be considered as legally binding within the United States.

The reproduction, transmission, and duplication of any of the content found herein, including any specific or extended information will be done as an illegal act regardless of the end form the information ultimately takes. This includes copied versions of the work both physical, digital and audio unless expressed consent of the Publisher is provided beforehand. Any additional rights reserved.

Furthermore, the information that can be found within the pages described forthwith shall be considered both accurate and truthful when it comes to the recounting of facts. As such, any use, correct or incorrect, of the provided information will render the Publisher free of responsibility as to the actions taken outside of their direct purview. Regardless, there are zero scenarios where the original author or the Publisher can be deemed liable in any fashion for any damages or hardships that may result from any of the information discussed herein.

Additionally, the information in the following pages is intended only for informational purposes and should thus be thought of as universal. As befitting its nature, it is presented without assurance regarding its prolonged validity or interim quality. Trademarks that are mentioned are done without written consent and can in no way be considered an endorsement from the trademark holder.

Introduction

Greetings! You have made a wonderful decision purchasing *Astrology Activated: Cutting Edge Insight Into the Ancient Art of Astrology (Understanding Zodiac Signs and Horoscopes)*. Thank you for doing so.

Most people worldwide have heard of astrology, and most people even know the basics of their astrology chart, but few have learned about the deeper mechanics of this ancient spiritual practice.

In short, astrology is the spiritual science of the motion and placement of the celestial bodies and how they determine things about us as spiritual beings and about our trajectory in life. This book will give beginners the tools they need to understand more about their own astrological makeup and learn how the behavior of the planets affects our world at large.

Today, astrology is used by people daily to give them guidance in their life to produce expectations about people's personalities and future events.

The following chapters will discuss all the elements involved in Astrology—the Sun and the planets that orbit around it and what effects they have on the signs they rule, the Houses of all the signs of the Zodiac, and their elements. Additionally, the natal chart, the Ascendant, and Moon signs and their impact on a person's chart are detailed.

There are plenty of books on this subject on the market; thanks again for choosing this one! Every effort was made to ensure it is full of as much useful information as possible. Please enjoy!

How to Get the Most Out of This Book

This book is written to work in a number of ways:

- Read this book in its entirety to enjoy the discoveries you will derive from the art of Astrology and learn how a natal chart is drawn, as well as how to find your Ascendant (rising sign) and the position of the Moon.
- Use this book as a guide to help you review and reread portions of it that may pertain to you, someone you know, or someone who is new in your life, especially if you and want to get an idea of who they are through their astrological Sun sign.
- To help you understand how to draw your natal chart, study where the planets were positioned at the time of your birth.
- Learn how to read your horoscope correctly and include the zodiac signs where your Ascendant and Moon are represented.

This book is written to be informative and instructional. Know that there are many variables affecting everyone's natal chart. The Zodiac sign that you are born under is where the Sun was positioned on the day of your birth.

Since your natal chart shows where the planets were when you were born, it will tell you the characteristics and tendencies that encompass who you are.

Astrology may be mysterious to some, but this book will shed some light on the subject. Also, this book is for you to enjoy!

The Planets

Chapter 1: The Celestial Bodies — The Planets Explained

The ancient origins of astrology were traced in the 18th Century B.C. in Mesopotamia by the Babylonian civilization. Many of the first astronomers were found in this civilization, and they studied astronomy, complementing this study with astrology. The Babylonians are credited with astrology's creation.

The Babylonian's modern astronomical measurement of minutes and seconds is derived from their system of numbers and the introduction of the concept of the zodiac. The astrological charts they created gave them the ability to predict seasons' change and particular celestial events that recurred each year. Because of the combination of their astrological charts and planetary movements, astronomy and astrology were considered the same science for 2,000 years.

In the 4th century B.C., the Greeks were introduced to Babylonian astrology. Through the studies of thinkers like Plato and Aristotle, astrology became a science that was highly regarded by the Greeks. In time, the Romans and Arabs adopted astrology. The names of the zodiac signs were given Roman names, which are still used today. The science of astrology expanded throughout the world

The Creation of the Zodiac

The Zodiac, meaning "circle of animals" in Greek, is believed to have begun in Egypt and later embraced by the Babylonians. The early astrologers were aware that the Sun would return to its initial position after it traveled over 12 lunar cycles.

Twelve constellations were connected to the progression of the seasons. Each constellation was assigned names of persons and animals. For example, the rainy season in Babylonia would occur when a specific constellation housed the Sun. This constellation was named for the water-bearer, Aquarius. However, do not be confused. Aquarius is an air sign, not a water sign. Subdivided into four groups, the signs of the Zodiac are:

- Air Signs: Aquarius, Gemini, Libra
- Earth Signs: Capricorn, Taurus, Virgo
- Fire Signs: Aries, Leo, Sagittarius
- Water Signs: Cancer, Scorpio, Pisces

Each group is recorded into its own group of "houses" on a circle. The division of the 12 houses is based on the Earth's daily rotation and relating to finances, relationships, travel, and the like. However, the 12 signs of the zodiac are divided based on the yearly rotation of the earth traveling around the sun.

They pertain to characteristics and areas of life, e.g., Mercury represents communication, cleverness, and wit, while the Moon is associated with motherly instincts and emotions, etc. The Sun and the Moon are associated with only one zodiac sign; the planets have two zodiac signs that they affect.

During this time, Babylonian astrologers considered the Sun, Moon, Mars, Jupiter, Mercury, and Venus to carry very specific powers. For example, Mars had a red color and was believed to be identified with war and aggression. (American Federation of Astrologers, 2019)

How the Celestial Bodies Affect Astrology

The planets are the most significant carriers of the role and destiny of a person's horoscope. Each has its own impact and identification of where they are at the time of a person's birth. The planets nearest to Earth have the strongest impact, and the planets farthest from Earth, known as transcendent planets, impact the person and the cumulative events at the time of their birth.

The Sun

The Sun is the core body around which all the other planets rotate. It is the most significant figure of the Universe. In astrology, the Sun is considered the special, central planet, although it is a star. Known as the God of all celestial spheres, the Sun is the symbol of cosmic consciousness and intelligence.

At the moment of birth, the Sun is the core essence of who you are, our conscious mind in Astrology. It offers life energy, vitality, and shines if it is well placed. Physical appearance, constitution, and health are especially affected and about how individuals present themselves to others and the type of energy they carry. It could be one that is courageous, dignified, and strong or one that is weak and indulgent.

The Sun portrays one's self, the way of being in the world. It can serve on different degrees, both the higher self and the ego.

Leo is ruled by the Sun and exalted in Aries.

It is the only star that is closest to the Earth at 92.96 million miles.

The Sun is our ego. It also controls our inner child. It makes the final decisions and reasons out things. It is our adult. Our basic identity and self-realization are the Sun.

The Sun is what we are learning to be. It is significant to realize that the Sun is the representation of reason rather than instinct. It reflects the present or "today and now," whereas the Moon is about the past in our lives through emotions.

Day of the week - The day of the week associated with the Sun is Sunday. It is associated with the eastern side of the world. Gold, rubies, and gemstones red in hue are related to the Sun.

The Sun in the body – brain, heart, head, bones, throat, mouth, lungs, spleen, arteries, blood, and circulation

Sun in business – the strength of the Sun will give an individual ruled by its energy the ability to do their best in their endeavors and the charisma that will draw everyone around them in a professional arena.

The Moon

While the Sun is who you are and dictates the zodiac personality, the Moon has the second most significant effect on your horoscope. The ebbs and tides caused by the Moon are known to people, and the biggest part is caused by gravity.

The Moon is a natural satellite of the Earth and is about 238,900 miles away. It is significant to astrology because the Moon is representative of the feminine principle. This principle is the most subtle and finest part of every human.

The Moon is all about your emotions and inner mood. The Moon is the ruler of Cancer, exalted in Taurus and weak in Scorpio and Capricorn. Eastern astrologers believe the Moon to be the most significant entity in each horoscope interpretation and understanding because it is our inner emotional world, our soul.

The Sun sign is easily known based on the day and month of your birth. However, the Moon sign is calculated by your date of birth, the time you were born, and the place of your birth.

The Moon orbits the Earth once every 27.322 days and visits each sign of the zodiac during its orbit. The Moon remains approximately two days in each sign. So, if on the day of your birth is when the Moon is about to enter the next sign, your time of birth is necessary to give you an accurate placement of the Moon in your chart. Exact times of birth are always favorable to chart, but an approximation of birth time can give an astrologer enough information to determine your Moon sign.

Day of the week - The day of the week associated with the Moon is Monday; its colors are white and silver, the gemstones are moonstone and pearls, and the side of the world is Southwest.

Moon in the body - breasts, ovaries, uterus, abdominal pain, and several psychological disorders

The Moon in business – natural sciences, army, archeology, psychology, and poetry

Mars

Mars rules the sign of Aries and Scorpio. The irony of this planet is that it is responsible for our first breath of life and our last breath on our death. This is indicated through the beginning of the zodiac circle with Aries, the sign of the infant, and the end of life in the sign of Scorpio, the sign of death.

Mars is linked with self-assertion and confidence, sexuality, energy, aggression, strength, impulsiveness, and ambition. The planet oversees competitions, physical activities, and sports in general.

Mars was honored as the mythological Roman god of war responsible for war, fights, and destruction and whose symbol is a symbol of a spear and shield. The soil of Mars and the human blood hemoglobin are rich in iron, which is why both share the deep red color.

The orbit of Mars around the Sun is 687 days and spends approximately 57.25 days in each zodiac sign. It's the first planet whose orbit is outside the Earth's orbit and does not set along with the Sun.

Day of the week - The day of the week associated with Mars is Tuesday. It occupies the south side of the world, and red is the color of the planet.

Mars in the body – the head, muscles, genitals, and prostate

Mars in business – surgeon, butcher, chemist, technician, hairdresser, engineer, electrician, and everything that relates to heavy machinery, tools, and hard work

Jupiter

Jupiter, next to the Sun, is the greatest body of our planetary system. Jupiter rules Pisces and Sagittarius and is associated with expansion, growth, good fortune, and prosperity. It governs foreign and long-distance travel, wealth, big business, religion, higher education, and the law. The urge for exploration and freedom, gambling, and the love of a party is associated with this planet.

Jupiter's orbit around the sun takes 11.9 years and spends 361 days, almost an Earth's year, in each zodiac sign. It is usually the fourth brightest object in the sky behind the Sun, Moon, and Venus.

Day of the week - Thursday is associated with Jupiter.

Jupiter in the body – hips, gall bladder, pancreas, liver, and upper legs

Jupiter in business – publishing, professors, politics, sports, advertising, diplomacy, banking, transport, energy, shipbuilding, tourism, and seafaring

The Romance languages (French jeudi, Spanish jueves, and Italian giovedi

Jupiter is related to the liberal art of geometry.

In ancient Roman mythology, Jupiter is a Roman god identical to Zeus, the supreme god of Greek mythology.

Saturn

Saturn is the planet that rules Capricorn. Saturn, in Roman mythology, is the god of crops, seeds, and agriculture. He is also the father and founder of civilizations and leader of titans, conformity, and social order.

In astrology, Saturn relates to precision, focus, ethics, nobility, civility, career, dedication, authority figures, stability, productiveness, hard lessons that are valuable, destiny structures, protective roles, balance, and karma (you reap what you sow). Saturn is also a part of the commitment, responsibility, and sense of duty. The rings of Saturn that surround and enclose the planet reflect the idea of human beings' limits.

Saturn takes 29.5 years to orbit around the Sun and spends approximately 2.46 years in each zodiac sign. In ancient Roman society, Saturn was worshipped as the most important and highest god among all other deities. He also shared the same level of worship with Jupiter.

Day of the week – The day of the week associated with Saturn is Saturday, and its colors are black and every shade of gray. The gems it corresponds to are amethyst, onyx, and blue sapphire.

Saturn in the body – bones, hair, teeth, rheumatism, arthritis, gallstones, loss of hair, and bone fractures

Saturn in business – geology, construction, history, mining, architecture, forestry, justice, dentistry, agriculture, and state affairs

Mercury

The planet that is closest to the Sun, Mercury, has a significant connection to it. Mercury is known as the messenger of the gods and is known for its swiftness and speed. It carries information from one person or level of existence to another.

Mercury is the ruler of both Gemini and Virgo and is exalted in Aquarius and is seen as our way of communicating and thinking.

The smallest planet in the Solar system is Mercury, and it is closest to the Sun at 35.98 million miles. Mercury is the planet of information and where our mind goes most of this life.

Mercury takes 88 days to orbit around the sun and only spends 7.33 days in each zodiac sign. This is the fastest orbit of any of the other planets.

Day of the week - The day of the week associated with Mercury is Wednesday. The gemstones that are governed by Mercury are emerald, peridot, green jade, tsavorite, chrome tourmaline, chrome diopside, and any other natural green gems.

Mercury in the body – lungs and nervous system

Mercury in business – languages, small business, sales, commercial, tourism, transport, accounting, printing industry, medicine, therapy, and job management

Venus

The most visible and brightest planet of the Solar system is Venus. Taurus and Libra are ruled by Venus. It is also exalted in Pisces.

In ancient Roman mythology, Venus is the goddess of beauty and love, and she is able to stir passions among the gods.

It rises and sets with the Sun and is known as the Morning star. This planet is particularly significant because of what it represents—the enjoyable and beautiful part of life that includes the excitement and desire for life, joy, pleasures, songs, love, the ability for people to love one another, and the ability to receive love. It is the dominance of the feminine.

The orbit of Venus around the Sun is 225 days and spends 18.75 days in each of the signs of the zodiac.

Day of the week – The day of the week associated with Venus is Friday. The colors are pink, white, and a mix of colors to exude colorfulness.

Venus in the body – skin, neck, reproductive organs, cheeks, and kidneys

Venus in business – art, fashion design, architecture, hair, and beauty, working with precious metals, jewelry, gems, decorative objects, and public affairs

Transcendental Planets

Uranus, Pluto, and Neptune are newly discovered planets. The last discovered planet was Pluto, which was seen in 1930.

Transcendental planets are significant in the natal business and common astrology.

Uranus

The astronomer William Herschel discovered Uranus in 1781. Attributed to the planet are eccentricity, originality, and unconventionality. The planet is always contrary to tradition, the old, archaic, and boring. Strong individuality and the ability to be completely different are awakened in an individual.

The October Revolution, the fall of the Bastille and other upheavals, the discovery of the steam locomotive, and the creation of the telegraphs and railways have occurred and are associated with Uranus.

Uranus is the co-ruler of Aquarius and exalted in the sign of Scorpio.

It takes 84 years for Uranus to circle the Zodiac. It is not visible to the naked eye.

Uranus in business – physics, nuclear physics, psychology, energy, cybernetics, internet, computers, telephones, aviation, electrical engineering, and engineering

Pluto

Originally known as Planet X, it was first searched by Percival Lowell, the mathematician, astronomer, and founder of the Lowell Observatory in Flagstaff, Arizona.

The first project initiating the search began in 1906. Before he could validate his search and confirm the discovery, Lowell died in 1916. The search for Planet X did not resume until 1929 by the then director of the Lowell Observatory, Melvin Sliefer. Sliefer teamed with Clyde Tombo, an astronomer from Kansas and spent the following year photographing the night sky, checking the photographs to detect if any of the photographed objects had moved from their place.

Pluto was officially discovered on February 18, 1930, and observed as a moving object on photographic plates that were taken a month earlier in January. Additional photos of Planet X were sent to the Harvard College Observatory to review and confirm the moving object's existence.

After Planet X's discovery, thousands of proposed names for the planet were sent to the Lowell Observatory. Venice Bernie, a young schoolgirl in Oxford, England, suggested naming the planet Pluto after the Roman god of the underworld. Bernie spoke about it in a conversation with her grandfather. In turn, he passed on the suggestion to Herbert Hall Turner, the director and astronomy professor at the University Observatory at Oxford, who then proposed the name to his colleagues in the United States.

The demonic and infernal system that led to the creation of concentration camps, slaughterhouses, and gas chambers came into being by the formation of the Third Reich almost immediately after the discovery of Pluto.

It takes 248 years to fully circle the Zodiac. It remains in each sign of the Zodiac between 15 and 26 years.

Pluto is the co-ruler of Scorpio and exalted in Leo. It is known to be the secret of life and death.

Pluto in business – criminology, politics, electronics, military science, banking, weapons, explosives pathology, underground construction, oil, psychotherapy, hypnosis, and computer technology

Neptune

The official discovery of Neptune was made by Johann Gottfried Galle in 1846 by using mathematic calculations of John Couch Adams and Urbain Le Verrier. This made the finding a British-French-German discovery. However, the first observer of this planet was the Italian astronomer Galileo Galilei in 1613.

Neptune is a blueish hued planet and was named after the Roman god of the sea.

The names of the planets were those of Roman gods, and the astronomers continued to name new planets using names in Roman mythology.

Neptune is the ruling planet of Pisces and is exalted in Cancer, along with Jupiter.

It takes Neptune 165 years to orbit the Sun and spends 13.75 years in each zodiac sign.

Neptune in the body - affects the nervous system and self-confidence

Neptune in business – art theory, theology, oceanography, chemicals, oil, pharmaceuticals, cosmetics, the perfume tobacco industry, music industry, coffee, and tea production, hotels, rest homes, spiritual centers, and film industry

The Astrological Wheel

The astrological wheel is where a diagram can be drawn to reveal a person's horoscope. The wheel is like a clock, divided into the 12 segments of the zodiac and runs counterclockwise.

The planet aligns with each sign of the zodiac at the time of an individual's birth. Wherever the Sun is at the moment of birth is the astrological zodiac sign of the person, followed by where the Moon and the person's ascendant (rising sign) is.

The *natal chart* of each individual is a diagram of the relative positions of planets and signs of the zodiac at a specific time (at one's birth) for use by astrologers in inferring individual character and personality traits and in foretelling events in a person's life.

The next chapter will identify each of the 12 signs of the Zodiac and their basic personality traits.

Signs of the Zodiac

Chapter 2: The 12 Signs of the Zodiac

The four parts of astrology include the planets and their orbit around the Sun, the signs of the Zodiac, the houses, and the aspects. Astrology is looked upon by astrologers as a gel of elements that complement the merging of these elements that make up the Universe. These elements synchronize and intertwine with one another in small and large ways.

The apparent annual path of the Sun's motion is called the ecliptic. This is the celestial sphere as seen from Earth. The Sun appears to move around the Earth's spin axis, which is tilted at 23.5° and lends to the seasonal variations in the amount of sunlight the earth receives on the surface. The other planets, except for Pluto, also orbit the Sun in pretty much the same plane.

Eight degrees on either side of the ecliptic is where you'll find the Zodiac. Its frequency and vibration allow people to express their behavior differently; how they live and how they express themselves are different as well.

Understanding the character of an individual's birth by determining the Zodiac signs and the meaning of specific planets found in the precise Zodiac sign the individual is born under gives an astrologer the ability to understand and create their natal chart accurately and authentically to read their fate.

Let's begin with the first sign of the Zodiac and work our way around the astrological wheel.

Aries (March 21-April 19) The Ram

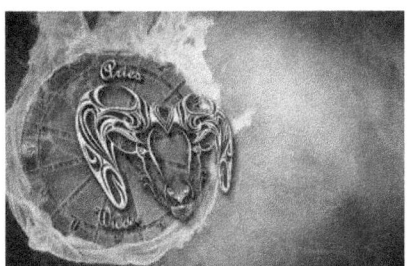

Zodiac Quality – Cardinal
Planet Ruler – Mars
Zodiac element - Fire
Gems – Diamonds, Coral and Amethyst

Aries is the Zodiac's first astrological sign. Its planetary ruler Mars makes Aries self-conscious, piercing, and courageous. People born under this sign sometimes overwork themselves.

Aries is indicative of dynamic, young, new, and animated. It is a cardinal sign with a fiery temperament. The sign is associated with the beginning of spring, a good time to begin new things.

Those born under the sign of Aries are determined, courageous, passionate, and determined. They are good in leadership roles. Their temperament can reveal impatience and impulsiveness. They can be and short-tempered and aggressive. As a Fire sign, Aries takes action, sometimes before mapping out a solid plan.

They may suffer from diseases of the head that can affect the blood vessels in the head and face. Migraines, neuralgia, insomnia, red cell problems and hair loss indicate this type of condition.

Aries in business - Aries is an engineer, bricklayer, welder, the new, the beginning, a hairdresser.

Compatibility – Best with Leo, Sagittarius, Aquarius, and Gemini

Celebrated Aries – Lady Gaga, Robert Downey, Jr., Hugh Hefner, Elton John, Leonardo da Vinci, Vincent van Gogh, Jackie Chan, Mariah Carey, CJ So Cool

Taurus (April 20-May 21) The Bull

Zodiac Quality – Fixed
Planet Ruler – Venus
Zodiac Element – Earth
Gems – Sapphire, Emerald, and Alabaster

Taurus is practical, stable, devoted, responsible, and reliable. It is the second sign of the Zodiac. Those born under this sign have an abundance of patience. Since their sign is a bull, one may think they are aggressive. However, quite the opposite is true.

Taurus can be peaceful and methodical. They desire peace that can be brought with a stable marriage, job, and organized life. This is about pacifism, and there are no dark or heavy feelings. This is the area where Taurus finds joy, happiness, romance, fertility, the gift of music, and the inclination to possess beautiful things.

Taurus can be seen as a fixed sign with energy that can't be changed. They can be slow to change and not open to new things (their other planetary aspects may alter this). They usually need more time to fully understand the problem. They can be slow to learn, but once they do, they retain what they learn.

They are a fixed, feminine sign whose element is earth. This also represents the allure of spring, pleasure, and all sorts of comfort. There is a desire for their life to be comfortable, pleasurable, and peaceful. Like the bull, they lay in the field, swatting the flies with their tail and left in solitude and peace.

They frequently suffer from illnesses of the neck, vocal cords, angina, tumors, diabetes, venereal disease, and diseases of the larynx, trachea, and thyroid.

Taurus in business – Taurus excels in natural sciences; one could be a banker, architect (with Libra and Capricorn), cook, and jeweler agriculture. He or she may be into botany, financial area, trade management, accessory design, construction, and cosmetics.

Compatibility – Capricorn, Cancer, Virgo, Pisces

Celebrated Taurus – Adele, Queen Elizabeth, Dwayne "The Rock" Johnson, George Clooney, William Shakespeare, Mark Zuckerberg, Michelle Pfeiffer, Cate Blanchett, George Lucas, Cher, Jack Nicholson, Kenan Thompson, Gigi Hadid

Gemini (May 21-June 20) The Twins

Zodiac Quality – Mutable
Planet Ruler – Mercury
Zodiac Element – Air
Gems – Citrine, Moonstone, Pearl, White Sapphire

Gemini, the twins, is complex, elusive, contradictory, and dual-natured. It is the third sign of the Zodiac. Their ruler, Mercury, is the planet of youth. Those born under Gemini seem to exhibit the behavior and fault of youth. They can be gentle, adaptable, curious, quick learners, and affectionate in their childlike demeanor.

Gemini love to speak to almost anyone, including strangers. They also love music, magazines, and books. They are great at adapting to social situations. Geminis enjoy travel as it gives them the ability to have new experiences and meet new people.

The negative side of Gemini is their craving to be the center of attention all the time. If the spotlight isn't on them, they'll leave. Relationships and friendships suffer because of this trait. Their desire to have the feeling of importance opens them to telling lies.

Physically, they frequently suffer from lung diseases, such as asthma and bronchitis.

Gemini in business - Publishing, literature, medicine (neuropathy, psychiatry, psychotherapy), technology, brokerage, painting, and journalism

Compatibility – Best with Aries, Libra, and Aquarius

Celebrated Gemini – Johnny Depp, Bob Dylan, Marilyn Monroe, Judy Garland, Paul McCartney, Chris Evans, Angelina Jolie, Prince, Venus Williams, Walt Whitman, Natalie Portman

Cancer (June 21-July 22) The Crab

Zodiac Quality – Cardinal
Planet Ruler – Moon
Zodiac Element – Water
Gems – Quartz, Crystal, Opal, Pearl

Cancer, the fourth sign of the Zodiac, is a water sign and ruled by the Moon. Those born under this sign are extremely intuitive and very sentimental. Of all the signs of the Zodiac, they are not the easiest to get to know. They have a great caring for their home and family and prefer to remain near those they know.

People born under the sign of Cancer are tenacious, extremely imaginative, persuasive, sympathetic, and very loyal. They are hobbyists, and they appreciate the arts, low-key meals with good friends, and relaxing near the water.

Cancers can be moody (remember they are ruled by the Moon—the ebb and flow of emotions), pessimistic, insecure, and manipulative.

When they're not in a mood, the "crabs" have a good sense of humor, sometimes, even offbeat to some. They make good listeners and have a healthy sense of empathy for the troubles of others. Cancers make outstanding friends, are dependable, reliable, and most definitely loyal.

Cancer rules the pulmonary part of the body and stomach. They are susceptible to mental problems and stomach illnesses.

Cancer in business - Nursing, politicians, interior decorators, horticulturists

Compatibility – Best with Virgo, Pisces, Scorpio, and Taurus

Celebrated Cancers – Meryl Streep, Robin Williams, Selena Gomez, Ariana Grande, Kevin Hart, Tom Hanks, Princess Diana, Tom Cruise, Giorgio Armani, Cyndi Lauper, Natalie Wood, Frances McDormand, Anjelica Huston

Leo (July 23-August 22) The Lion

Zodiac Quality – Fixed
Planet Ruler – The Sun
Zodiac Element – Fire
Gems – Ruby, Gold, Diamonds

Leo is the fifth sign of the Zodiac; it is a Fire sign ruled by the Sun. Leos are warm-hearted, humorous, creative, generous, and passionate. They are advocates of the arts and theater. They love having fun with their friends, camaraderie, and admiration from other people.

The lion is the realization of all the best traits of those born under this sign and is an apt symbol of this sign. Fire signs, such as Leo, draw people to them using their warm energy.

Leos are creative, the most dominant and spontaneous of all the signs in the Zodiac. Born leaders, they will either support or go against the status quo. Their personality is magnanimous, and that gives them a great presence.

On the negative side of the sign, Leos can be extravagant, and their personality can border on arrogance. If they become domineering, they can smother their relationships with friends and significant others. Leos are family- and community-oriented, and divorce can be especially disastrous and overwhelming for them.

Leos who are positive individuals are honest and decent people who will do the right thing regardless of the circumstance. They like to be organized, enjoy luxury, and are happy to share with others, so they can enjoy it as well.

Physically, Leos correspond to the heart, main arteries, spine, and back.

Leo in business - Actor, entertainer, announcer, advertising agent, artist, architect, business owner, comedian, DJ, event coordinator, hairstylist, financial planner, dancer, special education teacher, production artist, fashion designer

Compatibility – Best with Aries, Libra, Gemini, and Sagittarius

Celebrated Leos – Maya Rudolph, Helen Mirren, Jason Statham, Woody Harrelson, Robert De Niro, Jason Momoa, Robert Redford, Amy Adams, Madonna, Mila Kunis, Halle Berry, Chris Hemsworth

Virgo (August 23-September 22) The Maiden

Zodiac Quality – Mutable
Planet Ruler – Mercury
Zodiac Element – Earth
Gems – Carnelian, Moss Agate, Jade, Blue Sapphire

Virgo is the sixth sign of the Zodiac, ruled by Mercury. They are hardworking, practical, analytical, and loyal. They love animals and enjoy reading books, nature, and cleanliness.

They are always thinking, and they are detail-oriented and nurturing. They aren't opposed to being alone but enjoy the idea that someone needs and appreciates them, even from afar. Virgos are earth signs, and they apply that element to working with pottery or woodworking.

Neither loud nor bossy, they are incredibly good at developing strategies that make life easier and share it with anyone who sees the value. Virgos sometimes go overboard with work, and they take on more than they should.

One negative aspect of Virgos is their extreme attentiveness to their health and everyone else's. They are opinionated and will share their opinions with others regardless of whether they've been asked for their opinion or not.

If they think that the people around them are not doing their job efficiently or living up to their potential, they judge them, which can be a bit off-putting.

On Virgo's positive side, they love to laugh. They are kind, patient, and truly compassionate. They can be strong, silent types and think creatively. They revere family.

Physically, Virgos suffer from their nervous system, insomnia, stomach problems, intestines, and pancreas.

Virgo in business - Veterinarian, lab technician, nutritionist, office manager, environmental journalist, life skills coach

Compatibility – Best with Taurus, Cancer, Capricorn, and Scorpio

Celebrated Virgos – Beyoncé, Keanu Reeves, Paul Walker, Adam Sandler, Freddie Mercury, Pink, Selma Hayek, Sophia Loren, Mother Teresa

Libra (September 23-October 22) The Scales

Zodiac Quality – Cardinal
Planet Ruler – Venus
Zodiac Element – Air
Gems – Diamonds, Blue Sapphire, Emerald, White Marble

Ruled by the planet Venus, Libra is the seventh sign of the Zodiac. Libra is about balance as the symbol for their sign indicates. Of all the signs of the Zodiac, balance is what Libra needs more than any other sign.

The balance between family life, work, social, and recreation is what Libra would like to have—some time in their life. Libras take time to make up their minds to arrive at the right decision, and they seem a bit senseless to take so long to reach a decision.

They are the diplomats of the Zodiac, as they are cooperative, gracious, fair-minded, and social. When others are happy, they're happy, and they're the happiest when their world is balanced.

Libras can be charming, and they draw others to them. They meditate to help them find the balance that they need. A positive Libra is just and fair and becomes upset if a situation isn't that way.

The negative side of Libras is they take just about forever to make a decision, frustrating anyone who's waiting for them to make one. It may appear to others that they're absent-minded or even lazy. If a situation seems unjust or unfair to them, they will argue about the situation. Libras do not like confrontation in the form of family scenes or violence.

Libras are associated with the kidneys, urinary tract, and reproductive organs. They can also have sensitive blood vessels and skin. They frequently suffer from inflammation of the urogenital organs and diabetes.

Libra in business - Graphic designer, human resources, makeup artist, lawyer, set designers, musicians, photographers, models, actors, and public figures

Compatibility – Best with Leo, Sagittarius, Gemini, and Aquarius

Celebrated Libras - Mahatma Gandhi, John Lennon, Simon Cowell, Snoop Dog, Emilia Clarke, Gwen Stefani, Carrie Fisher, Kate Winslet, Serena Williams

Scorpio (October 23-November 21) The Scorpion

Zodiac Quality – Fixed
Planet Ruler – Mars, Pluto
Zodiac Element – Water
Gems – Aquamarine, Coral, Topaz, Obsidian, Beryl, Apache Tear

Scorpio is the Mars-ruled eighth sign of the zodiac. Scorpio's element is water, but, unlike Pisces and Cancer, the water is hot. Astrologers consider that the sign is more connected to Pluto, which recently lost its planet status.

Scorpio is a water sign that is passionate, stubborn, brave, resourceful, and someone who can be a true friend. Long-term friendships, the truth, and teasing those who they know will not take offense are things that this sign appreciates.

The scorpion that represents this sign isn't aggressive until someone aggravates and provokes them. Even after someone does irritate them, they would rather not fight but be contemplative about the situation. They are secret-keepers and intensely feel emotion more than any other sign. This gives Scorpio the ability to get to the bottom of any issue or situation and help people.

On the negative side, Scorpios have a streak for inflicting revenge on someone. Scorpios do not forget those who have wronged them and often hold a grudge.

On the positive side, the self-control that Scorpios have in practically every other part of their lives is admirable. Because they are so self-controlled, they expect others to emulate them. They are disciplined, protective, and giving and expect to receive the same from others.

Scorpio in business - Financial advisor, physician, engineer, researcher, psychologist, pharmacist, marketing associate, market analyst, occupational therapist

Compatibility – Best with Pisces, Virgo, Cancer, and Capricorn

Celebrated Scorpios - Grace Kelly, Indira Gandhi, Scarlett Johansson, Jodie Foster, Leonardo DiCaprio, Bill Gates, Matthew McConaughey, Ryan Gosling, Pablo Picasso

Sagittarius (November 22-December 21) The Archer

Zodiac Quality – Mutable
Planet Ruler – Jupiter
Zodiac Element – Fire
Gems – Ruby, Sapphire, Turquoise, Topaz, Amethyst

Those born under the fire sign of Sagittarius are ruled by Jupiter. Sagittarius is the ninth sign of the Zodiac. Sagittarians are creative, adventurous, and happy. They have a love for travel, meeting new people, and learning new things. They are idealistic and generous, and they have a good sense of humor.

Mundane or normal routines are not for this Fire sign. They can become restless if they are not dealing with variety. Their love of traveling and adapting to new experiences makes them a lot of fun. They have an abundance of friends.

On the negative side of this sign, a confined Sagittarius will bring out a rude and uncooperative fire sign. They rarely follow through with plans that border the grandiose because they are easily sidetracked.

On the positive side of Sagittarius, they are intelligent, and being around like-minded intelligent people is an enjoyable experience for them. They are spiritually inclined and creative. Sagittarians will travel to places to seek enlightenment in all ways.

Sagittarius dominates the buttocks and thighs and can suffer from numerous and varied weaknesses, depending on the rest of the horoscope and its aspects.

Sagittarius in business - Uber driver, tourism specialist, freelance writer, environmental engineer, publisher, international travel consultant

Compatibility – Best with Aquarius, Leo, Aries, Aquarius

Celebrated Sagittarians – Richard Pryor, Steven Spielberg, Miley Cyrus, Brad Pitt, Jay-Z, Zoë Kravitz, Kaley Cuoco, Jane Fonda, Bruce Lee, Winston Churchill, Jimi Hendrix, Ludwig van Beethoven

Capricorn (December 22-January 19) The Goat

Zodiac Quality – Cardinal
Planet Ruler – Saturn
Zodiac Element – Earth
Gems – Ruby, Agate, Garnet, Black Onyx

Saturn ruled Capricorn is the tenth sign of the Zodiac and an Earth sign. Capricorn's symbol of a goat is significant, as it represents this sign's aim to climb higher. Capricorn is successful, regardless of any odds they may face. They are extremely goal-oriented. They work hard in order to reach their goals. Capricorn is self-disciplined, with a penchant to be a teacher or scientist. They also make good managers.

Music, family, and anything made well and are of quality are enjoyed by Capricorns. They take their life and career seriously because they are on a mission to achieve their goals. They tend to be intolerant of people who do not show the same respect for their own lives.

On the negative side, their effort to achieve their goals may seem boring to others. Capricorn people sometimes give the impression that they lack emotion; they can be stingy and selfish. They will refuse to see a situation for what it is and that they may be wrong about it. If there is anything that a Capricorn dislikes immensely, it is being wrong.

On the positive side, they make solid, realistic, and logical decisions. They're good at being able to see the bottom line. They have a dry sense of humor that, at times, borders on sarcasm. They are also family-oriented. They are extremely intelligent and do very well with analysis and numbers.

The total skeletal system, knees, and bones are ruled by Capricorn.

Capricorn in business - CEO, business analyst, architect, creative director, financial planner, copywriter, intelligence analyst, human resources manager

Compatibility – Virgo, Scorpio, Pisces, and Taurus

Celebrated Capricorns – Betty White, Dolly Parton, LeBron James, Julia Louis-Dreyfus, Muhammad Ali, Michelle Obama, David Bowie, Mary J. Blige, Elvis Presley, Martin Luther King, Jr.

Aquarius (January 20-February 18) The Water Bearer

Zodiac Quality – Fixed
Planet Ruler – Uranus
Zodiac Element – Air
Gems – Amethyst, Garnet, Moss Agate, Opal, Magnet

Aquarius is ruled by Uranus and is the eleventh sign of the Zodiac. Some Aquarians take delight in saying they are ruled by Uranus because they consider themselves originals and eccentrics and associate themselves with other qualities we find distinctive in individuals.

Although the symbol for this sign is a water-carrier, Aquarius is an air sign and considered rational, social, and communicative individuals. They are very intellectual and friendly.

Aquarians may seem to be detached emotionally as a friend to others. However, when you get to know them better, you'll find they are more involved emotionally on a deeper level and make for a true friend. Individuals born under this sign tend to be comedic and will look to cheer people up from any issue or sadness they may have.

Although Aquarians appreciate significant relationships with others, they are extremely independent. They flourish in their freedom and thrive on the ability to come and go anytime they please. Aquarians, without their freedom, is like being deprived of oxygen. Trying to tie them down or restrict them will make them flee. This is not the most free-spirited sign in the Zodiac, yet they certainly enjoy having freedom more than most.

Aquarians can be incredibly stubborn. This personality trait does not bode well at times and can lead to relationship and career failures. Even if there are a multitude of documentation that proves them wrong, they will stick to doing things their own way.

Although they are stubborn and often rebuff the evidence that finds fault in their own conclusions, they don't impose their ideas on others. Aquarians have great respect for other people's ideas and opinions, and they have the ability to understand the differences and views of others.

On the negative side, they can become resentful and depressed if they don't have enough time to be alone with themselves. Aquarians engage in self-rumination, habits, and activities that may seem to others as eccentric. They indulge themselves by working on their hobby.

Aquarians' demeanor may seem standoffish, and it takes quite a bit for them to be pushed over the edge. They will hold in whatever it is that bothers them until they can no longer deal with the situation, at which point, they'll explode and lose control.

On the positive side of this sign, they are probably one of the friendliest of all other signs of the Zodiac. They do well in networking with others and make friends wherever they go. Aquarians are at ease in speaking with other people they may have just met, but they make the other person feel like they've known each other for years.

They do need time to be alone, and they do well with yoga or meditation. Their quiet observations of other people and events may be a surprise when conversing about their viewpoints and opinions with others. At times, they have a view that is slanted and that others may not have considered or thought about.

Aquarians tend to suffer from the nervous system, circulation, and heart disease.

Aquarius in business – Research scientist, inventors, electronics, social networking, pilot, professor of physics or astronomy, computer programmer

Compatibility – Libra, Gemini, Aries, and Sagittarius

Celebrated Aquarians – Sharon Tate, Farrah Fawcett, Abraham Lincoln, Oprah Winfrey, Bob Marley, Lisa Marie Presley, Christian Bale, Mariska Hargitay, Harry Styles, Yoko Ono, Paul Newman, James Dean, Dr. Dre, Chris Rock

Pisces (February 19-March 20) The Fish

Zodiac Quality – Mutable
Planet Ruler – Neptune, Jupiter
Zodiac Element – Water
Gems – Amethyst, Aquamarine, Bloodstone, Jade, Sapphire

Pisces, the twelfth sign of the Zodiac, is ruled by Jupiter. Some astrologers believe that those born under this sign are affected by Neptune.

Pisceans are extremely popular with just about anyone because they are even-tempered and relaxed by nature. They are less threatening to others they associate with. Pisceans are empathetic, compassionate, caring, highly emotional, and faithful individuals. They also tend to be more involved and caring about other people's problems instead of dealing with their own.

Pisces individuals prefer to spend time alone and withdraw into other worlds of their creation. They can be who they want to be and do anything they want to do in these worlds. They have a deep appreciation for art, and they travel to exotic places.

The negative side of Pisces is, due to their emotional makeup, they absorb the emotions of others to the point of falling ill, and they are fearful of making any decisions. They don't want to disagree with others, so they avoid making any decisions at all.

Pisces can be absent-minded and need a nudge every now and again to complete projects and tasks they begin. Managerial positions are not ones Pisces do well in, although this can be affected by other aspects of their horoscope.

The positive side of Pisces shows them to have empathy for the problems of others and reach out to those who are in need. They care deeply and may not exhibit their feelings on the surface. Pisces are empathetic, musically inclined, and have a deep understanding of human weaknesses.

Pisces rules the feet, and they may suffer from bone spurs and bruising of the feet. They also have respiratory and circulatory problems as well. Their psyche is very sensitive, so they withdraw and isolate themselves from others.

Pisces in business - Production editor, graphics designer, physical therapist, filmmaker, mental health technician, photographer, human resources coordinator

Compatibility – Cancer, Scorpio, Taurus and Capricorn

Celebrated Pisces – Michelangelo, Albert Einstein, Gloria Vanderbilt, Sophie Turner, Stephen Curry, Rihanna, Steve Jobs, Johnny Cash, Kurt Cobain, George Harrison, Daniel Craig

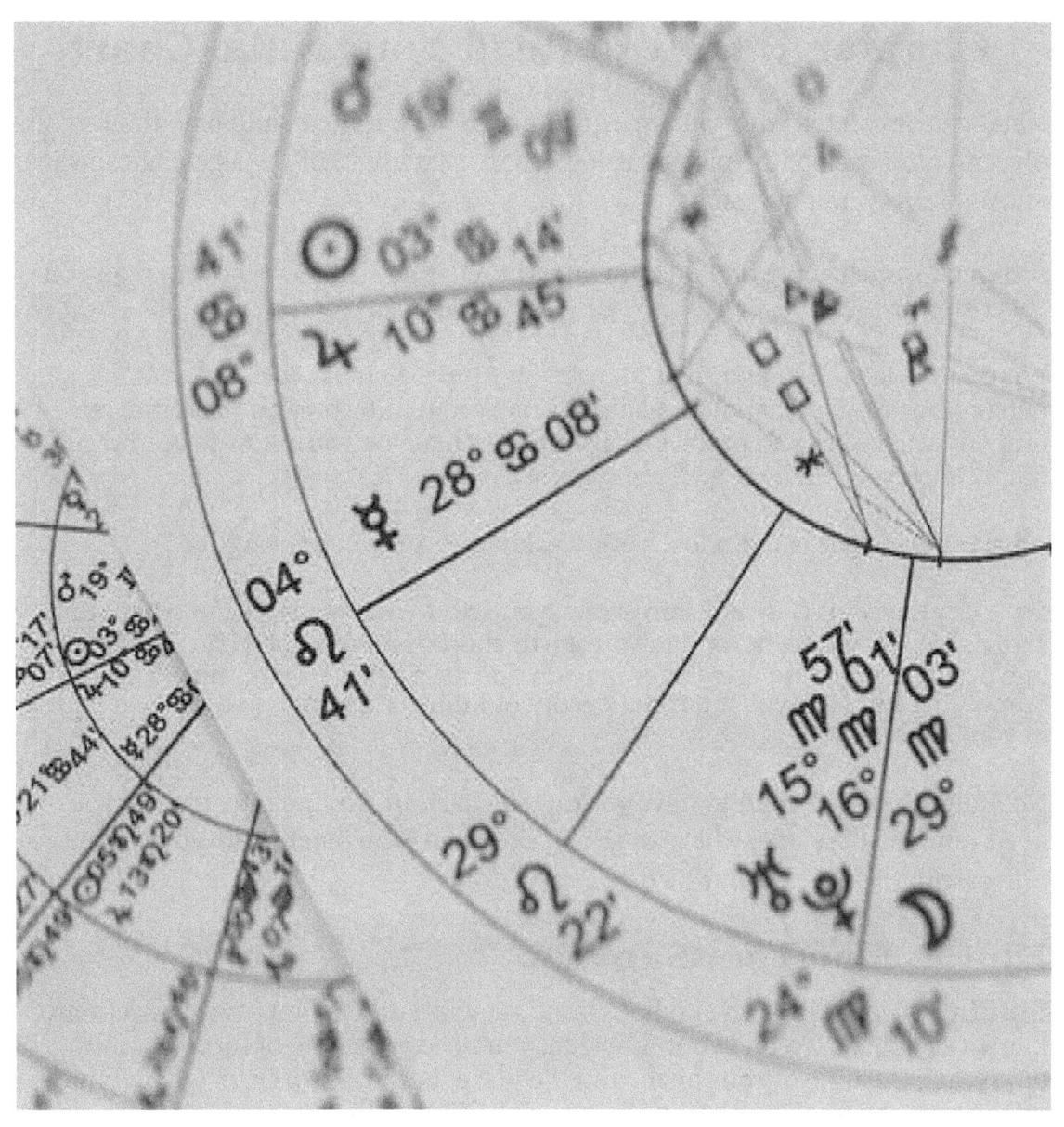

Your Natal Chart

Chapter 3: How to Read Your Natal Chart

Natal charts can tell who you are, the Sun sign of your birth, and how the placement of each of the planets is located in each house of the astrological wheel affects your overall persona.

Although some people find it confusing, this chapter will cover how to read your chart step-by-step.

Your natal chart, also known as an astrology birth chart, is the study of personality, the stars, and the planets. It is used to interpret and illustrate an individual's nature and predict their future. When you learn how to read your natal chart, you will have a view of yourself.

An astrology chart can disclose your weaknesses and your strengths.

So, every day you read your horoscope, you know your sun sign and compatible sign as well. If you've never had your birth chart done, it's not a bad idea to have one drawn for you. An astrologer may do one for a price, or you can get it online. Some sites will have you enter the pertinent information and give you an analysis of your chart.

No matter how you want to have your natal chart drawn, the information you need remains the same, where the Sun, Moon, and the planets are aligned in the universe at the time of your birth.

How to Find Your Sun Sign

Finding your sign – The Zodiac chart is a wheel divided into twelve sections, known as houses. To find your Sun sign, you need your date of birth (month/day/year), the time of your birth, and the place. Your date of birth will fall into one of the sections. The section that your birthdate falls into is your Zodiac sign.

An example of this is January 28, 1947, 8:45 p.m. in New York, New York. This birthdate falls into the sign of Aquarius, whose astrological sign dates are January 20-February 18. This determines the Sun sign.

The meaning of your Sun sign – The influence on your personality is influenced by your Zodiac sign. As an example, if you're born under the sign of Aquarius, you are a good friend, have a sense of humor, are extremely independent, and can be stubborn at times.

The information about the association of your personality traits with your Zodiac sign can be found in an astrology book that can be purchased online or at your local bookstore. You can also try your local library for books on astrology.

What affects how your Sun sign is read – The determination of your Zodiac sign is just one element of how your natal chart can be read. Various aspects influence the chart. The houses and planets need to be considered to get a full reading of your natal chart. That information is deemed from the date of your birth and the place where you were born.

The Astrological House – Do not confuse the Houses with the Zodiac wheel; they are not the same.

The Zodiac wheel rotates annually based on the yearly rotation of the Sun. The Houses represent the Earth's rotation on its axis, which happens in a 24-hour rotation.

The natal planets (birth signs) in the birth chart are stationary, while the planets that rotate around the Sun (the Moon, Mercury, Saturn, Mars, Jupiter, and Venus and transcendental planets of Uranus, Neptune, and Pluto) consistently rotate in the Universe and move across the Houses.

Astrologers fuse the two systems when they draw a natal chart. It tells what a person's Sun sign is from the Zodiac, as well as identifies the person's personality traits.

To put it simply, a certain period of life will exemplify the essence of that House. We follow the sun's 365-day cycle and go through a solar cycle each year of all the Houses.

Your time of birth is crucial when your chart is being calculated. There is a shift every four minutes in the Houses, so even if individuals are born on the same day, their natal charts will be entirely different. This is based on whether they were born in the morning or the evening.

Houses in a natal chart reflect the different facets of an individual's life based on location and birth time. They will interpret the obstacles or gifts you will face in life. Each planet, celestial point, or asteroid "lives" within a House. The placement of the planets gives you information about you, as well as how you synchronize with the world around you. As planets move in the Universe across these domains, distinctive embodied events, as well as emotional ones, are triggered. (Faragher, 2018)

So, an accurate time of birth can make all the difference in your natal chart. The chart will be inaccurate if your time is incorrect.

What the Houses Tell Us

Looking at your chart for the first time, it may seem to be a confusing compilation of symbols and lines across the face of the astrological wheel. Your focus is scattered, and it's not easy to know where you need to look first. Some areas have a number of symbols, some grouped together, while other areas have no symbols at all. Why is a portion of the natal chart blank? What are these symbols, and what do they mean? (Faragher, 2018)

Being able to read a natal chart is pretty uncomplicated. You just have to know where you need to begin. In order to begin, you need to locate the anchor of the chart, the Ascendant. The Ascendant in a chart is also known as the rising sign and is located at the furthest left point of the center horizon line. This discloses the zodiac sign that was materializing from the eastern horizon at the exact time of your birth. (Faragher, 2018)

The Sun brings to light our truth. The Moon is our emotional makeup, and the Ascendant exposes our landscape. Examples of the kind of landscape we're dealing with are one of independence and nonconformity that defines an Aquarius Ascendant, and security, stability, and loyalty will define a Taurus Ascendant.

The Ascendant reveals the ruling planet of the natal chart. Someone with an Aquarius Ascendant is ruled by the precise Saturn, while the romantic Venus rules a Taurus Ascendant.

Locating the Ascendant

The Ascendant needs to learn how the houses will be labeled in the natal chart.

The Zodiac wheel can be looked at as a clock. You read this clock counterclockwise. Your Ascendant is located at the horizontal line that cuts across the "clock," so you will find your Ascendant at the 9 o'clock position. This position indicates the cusp of the First House.

The Astrological Houses Defined

The first six houses indicated the different facets of your life.

First House - The First House reflects you at the time of your birth, your physical appearance, temperament, attitude, and other qualities inherent in your makeup. Your personality is tremendously influenced by the sign and planets that are found in the First House.

Second House – This house is where your self-worth, money, personal assets, and your attitude toward these aspects in your chart are represented. How secure you will be financially and your well-being emotionally over the course of your life can be gauged by what planet and sign are found in this house. (wikiHow Staff, 2019)

Third House – Communication and transportation are represented by the Third House. The physical forms of communication, like email, text, or letters, are under this house. Also, traveling short distances and how others communicate with you are included. This also indicates how you learn, manner of speech, self-expression, and your mental attitude.

Fourth House – Family, home, property, your childhood, and internal emotions that correlate with these areas are represented in the Fourth House.

Fifth House – How you connect with children and relate to them are aspects of the Fifth House. Love affairs and romance are also part of the Fifth House. It shows how you have fun and approach things that bring you pleasure.

Sixth House – Your physical health and well-being throughout your life is represented in the Sixth House.

Along with the first six houses, there are six additional houses to round up all the information you can derive from your natal chart.

Seventh House – Committed, serious relationships are represented in the Seventh House. This house rules romantic partnerships and marriage. It can tell you what you need to have a long-term partner in the romance department.

Eighth House – This is the house of rebirth and transformation. Sex, birth, death, injuries, surgeries, decay, and healing are represented in this house.

Ninth House – This house represents travel that is long distance. The journeys found in the Ninth House are both metaphorical and physical. Journeys of over 500 miles, transformations, and emotional journeys are in the Ninth House.

Tenth House – Your career, status, aspirations, and ambitions are found in the Tenth House. Your place in a community is revealed in this house.

Eleventh House – The Eleventh House represents if and when your dreams will come true and is known as the house of hopes.

12th House – This is the house of secrets, hidden emotions, and secret aspects of a person's past; all things that are hidden are exposed in the 12th House. (wikiHow Staff, 2019)

How the Planets Play a Part in the Natal Chart

Finding the planets – The planets are found throughout the chart with different symbols representing them. Your reading is affected by the planets that pass through the different houses of your chart.

The First Set of Planets Are *Personal Planets*

The Personal planets are the planets whose orbits are closest to Earth's orbit, and therefore closest to our physical being.

Sun – The Sun is indicated by a circle with a dot in the center of the chart. It is a personal planet that represents a person's purpose and identity.

Moon - A half-crescent moon shape reflects on the events that a person experiences in their life and how they react.

Venus – Venus is the symbol for women. It's a personal planet and represents what you are comfortable with and what you enjoy.

Mars - Mars is the male symbol. The planet represents your actions and will.

Mercury - Mercury is the symbol of the female but with two small lines at the top of the circle. The planet represents your capacity to perceive and relate to objects and individuals.

The Second Set of Planets Are Outer Planets

The **outer planets** move very slowly through the signs of the Zodiac. Sometimes it takes up to 15 years to complete a transit.

Jupiter – The symbol resembles the number 4 and represents how you assimilate with society and your personal growth

Saturn–This planet is represented by a symbol that resembles the number 5. It also represents the rules you create for yourself over your life, as well as your personal responsibilities

Uranus, Pluto, and Neptune each have symbols that are relatively complex, representing them.

Uranus – The symbol resembles the female symbol turned upside down. This planet represents your ability to learn and grow.

Neptune – The symbol is an upside-down cross with two lines on each side and loops up. This planet indicates to your imagination and ideas.

Pluto – The symbol for this planet is a combination of Uranus and Neptune: a female symbol, facing upward and two lines on each side that loop up. Pluto is your capability for inner growth and change, denoting a deep and personal type of change.

Understanding and Interpreting Your Chart

To read your natal chart precisely, you need to consider where the planets appear. Where does the planet appear? In what house? Under which sign? Once you address these questions and acquire the information, you will get insight into your life path and personality.

The *Planets* describe what you enjoy and what it is that drives you. The *Houses* illustrate how and your manner of completing a given task. The *Signs* display in what areas you can foresee certain aspects of change or growth in your life. (wikiHow Staff, 2019)

If you are not experienced in drawing an astrological chart, there are websites that will generate one for your use. All sites are not accurate, so take care in choosing the site you want to use. Read reviews and feedback from other users to get an idea as to how good the site is. It's possible to find a professional astrologer in your area who can create a chart for you.

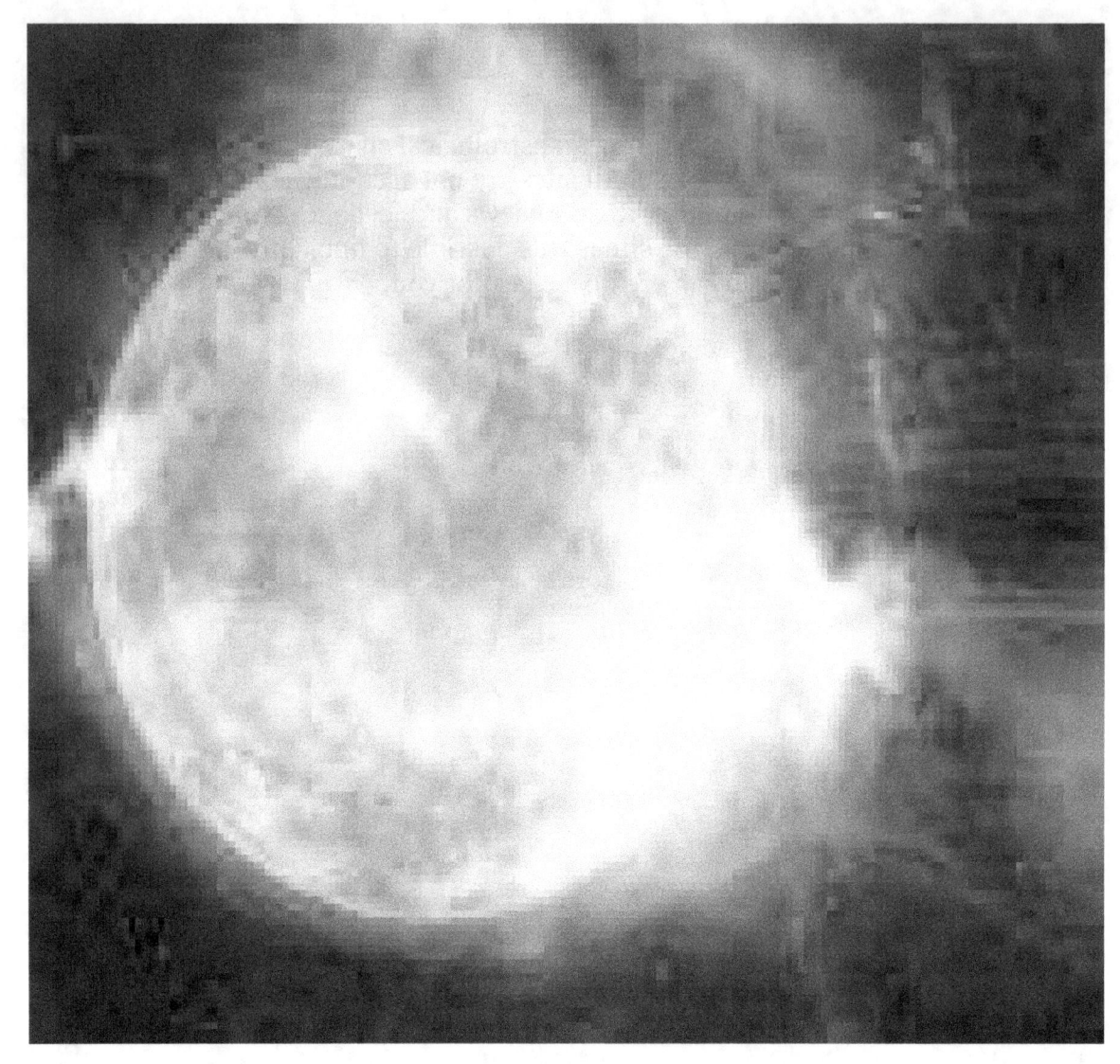

Your Sun Sign and You

Chapter 4: Your Sun Sign and You

Now that you know how your astrological chart is mapped using the Planets, Houses, and your Zodiac sign, let's concentrate on your Sun sign, the Zodiac sign you were born under.

As you've read in the previous chapters, your Sun sign is what dictates your zodiac personality. Your Sun sign is easily determined by the month, day of your birth, and the position of the Sun. For instance, a person's sun sign would be Taurus if the constellation Taurus was behind the Sun at the time of their birth. (Napier, Beth, 1995)

Know that the Sun sign in Astrology is the beginning, the tip of the iceberg. The study can take you into the mysteries that are deep within the universe. Yet, it all begins with the Sun, and that is what this chapter will cover.

These astrological outlines for each sign of the Zodiac are a general overview of each sign. Each of us has different aspects that were in play at the time of our birth, so the influence of other planets will tell other parts of your Astrological Chart.

Sun Signs in Astrology and Their Meaning

The sun sign is what describes your nature and personality traits. These traits remain constant throughout all the phases of life. Regardless of what happens, it is the image that all you get to know and see. It comes from the deepest, truest part of you. At the center of the Solar System is the Sun, which is a star. Like the sun, your sun sign illustrates the personal center that is uniquely you.

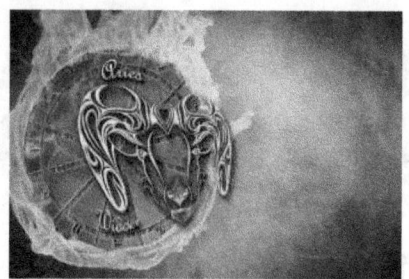

Aries (March 21-April 20
The Ram

Aries is ruled by Mars, the first sign of the Zodiac and is a Fire sign. The best words to describe an Aries are confident, determined, optimistic, and passionate. They also exhibit a good amount of courage when needed.

Aries do well in managerial and leadership roles and enjoy physical challenges and individual sports. They also can display impatience and impulsiveness. They can also be short-tempered. If they don't use their talents, the possibility of not finding their path in any role or job is unfortunately real.

March 21st is the spring equinox, the beginning of the new zodiac year, and new beginnings. This is what Aries represents. The Ram is impulsive, ambitious, energetic, and adventurous.

They can create new ideas that they put into action immediately. They are intelligent and are not afraid to take on new challenges head-on. They may become agitated if the ideas they implement do not show immediate results.

Aries is compatible with Aquarius, Leo, Sagittarius, and Gemini.

Taurus (April 21-May 20
The Bull

The second sign of the Zodiac, Taurus, falls under the element of earth and is ruled by Venus. Those born under the sign of Taurus are devoted, stable, practical, reliable, and responsible. This is a very steady sign and is patient as well.

Although the bull is the symbol of this sign, people may be under the impression that Taurus is aggressive. Contrary to this belief, Taurus is peaceful and methodical. Their actions are deliberate, yet they are relaxed.

Taurus enjoys the sensual things of life, including food, luxury, and sex; everything that is luxurious is welcomed by this sign. Their luxury is the result of hard work. They enjoy cooking, music, quality in their surroundings, and gardening. Complications in their life or work environment, sudden change, and insecurity are things that Taurus does not welcome.

Well-balanced and stable, Taurus obeys the law, loves peace, and works to maintain their luxury. They have a strong aversion to being in serious debt, and they do everything they can to maintain their sense of security.

Taurus is astute and more practical than intellectual. They are known to formulate an opinion, and once it's established, it will remain unchanged, even if it's against the tide of popular consensus. Holding on to their ideals makes Taurus steadfast and true to their beliefs. They can keep cool during difficult times.

Their downside is their stubbornness and unchanging ideals that they adopt. This can make them challenging to get along with. Although they value the law and adhere to it, they may sabotage an authority figure if they feel their leadership is lacking.

On a positive note, this sign finishes what they begin. Leaving a project or task undone is rare. They make decisions that are usually the right ones due to their practice of deliberate thinking. Taurus enjoys spending time with loved ones and is family-oriented.

Taurus is compatible with Capricorn, Cancer, Pisces, and Virgo.

Gemini (May 21-June 29)
The Twins

This twin sign is complex, contradictory, elusive, and dual-natured. Gemini is the third sign of the Zodiac; its element is Air, and it is ruled by Mercury.

Those who are born under this sign have a tendency to display the faults and behavior of the young as Mercury is the planet of youth.

Gemini has a childlike quality to them, making them curious, affectionate, and gentle. It also has them acting indecisive, nervous, and inconsistent. A Gemini loves speaking with everyone and anyone, total strangers included. They also appreciate books, magazines, and music.

Geminis are happy in groups, sharing concepts and ideas, having purposeful conversations, or going out to have fun. They rarely do anything alone. Social situations are their forte, and their love of talking with people makes their time socializing all the more pleasurable for them.

This sign is adventurous and carefree and enjoys traveling. It gives Gemini new opportunities to meet new people and acquire new knowledge.

Gemini's love to be excited intellectually, and they delve into the spiritual, mental, and physical arenas enthusiastically. Their personalities can be described as airy and breezy, which draws people to them. They love new experiences and will, at times, have them alone, though being alone is not the norm for this sign.

Gemini's negative side is that they must be at the center of attention at all times. If they aren't, and the attention is being paid elsewhere, they will leave the event, friendship, relationship, career, or party; you get the idea. Feeling important is a strong need for Geminis.

This sign tends to tell little white lies. Gemini will be rude and lack empathy when they focus only on themselves.

The positive side of Gemini is that they are charming, great conversationalists, and are interesting to be around. They are optimists and very funny. They hate to be bored, so they make their own enjoyment and fun to avoid the humdrum.

Gemini is compatible with Leo, Libra, Aries, and Aquarius.

Cancer (June 21-July22
The Crab

The Moon rules the water sign of Cancer, the fourth sign of the Zodiac. They are sentimental, sensitive, and emotional, and they care immensely for their home and family. They are profoundly intuitive and prefer to be near those who they know.

Tenacious, persuasive, sympathetic, and loyal, Cancers also have a great imagination. Hobbies are their favorite, and they enjoy doing them at home. They have an appreciation for art, and they love relaxing near water and getting together with good friends for quiet dinners and social events.

Cancers can be pessimistic, moody, insecure, and manipulative.

The symbol for Cancer, the crab, personifies this sign because the crab's shell is carried on its back. Cancers are loyal to family and friends and remain close to home, and are all about what revolves in their home. Their friends and family are their circles, and they tend to be dedicated to them. When a Cancer finds something that makes them happy, they will grab onto it.

Cancers like to be needed and feel secure in someone's love and caring. The best qualities of this sign are protective instincts and bravery. They do become moody and reclusive if their needs aren't met. They have a nurturing streak and are quite gentle with family and friends.

The negative side of Cancer is the tendency to be insecure, clinging to things and people. They can be moody, too, especially if they think a relationship is being lost. They will lie, although rarely. The lies are their feeling of insecurity about being alone.

Cancer is compatible with Taurus, Virgo, Pisces, and Scorpio.

Leo (July 23-August 22
The Lion

Leo is ruled by the Sun; it is the fifth sign of the Zodiac and is a fire sign. Those born under this sign are generous, humorous, creative, and passionate. They get enjoyment from holidays, theater, fun with friends, and the admiration of others, and they love bright colors.

The lion is a fitting symbol for this sign because the lion is the epitome of the regal. Leos are warm individuals, and they use that energy to attract people who can't help but gravitate to them. People who are close to them feel loved and appreciated.

Like the lion who is the king of the jungle, Leo is the most creative, spontaneous, and dominant sign of the entire Zodiac. Positive, self-confident, and strong-willed, they are born leaders who can either support or revolt against any circumstances or a state of affairs.

Their charitable and selfless personality affords them a presence that is commanding. They get a tremendous amount of loyalty from those who work with them and are rather uncomplicated individuals.

Leo's negative side has their arrogance on display if their sense of self-worth becomes greater than what it really is. They need to express themselves in a domineering manner, smothering their friends and significant others, but they need to be in charge is one of their faults. Those who don't understand a Leo may decide to leave. Family is very important to them, and divorce or loss of relationships or community can be very devastating and overwhelming to them.

The positive Leo is honest and decent and will do the right thing regardless of the circumstance. They excel in organizing, and they enjoy luxury. They also like the people whom they love and who are closest to them to enjoy the luxury as well. They are open to everyone, at least when they first meet them, and develop relationships. Some of these relationships become lifelong associations.

Leos are compatible with Libra, Sagittarius, Aries, and Gemini.

Virgo (August 23-September 22
The Maiden

The Earth sign, Virgo, is ruled by Mercury and is the sixth sign of the Zodiac. Loyal, practical, kind, analytical, and hardworking, Virgo likes to connect with animals, enjoy nature, books, and everything that is clean!

Virgos are calm and collected, which is why the maiden was chosen to represent Virgo. On the surface, like a maiden, they appear to be calm and mild-mannered. However, there is a myriad of activity that is ongoing. They're always on the go; they never stop thinking and are always analyzing and assessing their situations.

They are extremely detail-oriented.

Virgos are nurturing individuals and don't mind spending time alone, as long as they know that someone appreciates and needs them. Virgos are not loud or overbearing and enjoy strategizing.

Virgo's negative side has them being too attentive to the health of others, as well as their own; they can be somewhat obsessive about it. They can be judgmental and opinionated and will share their opinions regardless if they're asked or not.

On the positive side, Virgos are extremely compassionate when it comes to others, patient, and kind, and they always enjoy a good laugh. They're creative thinkers and can sometimes be strong, silent types. Family is always important to them.

Virgo is compatible with Capricorn, Taurus, Cancer, and Scorpio.

Libra (September 23-October 22)
The Scales

Libra is the seventh sign of the Zodiac, an Air sign represented by the symbol of the scales and ruled by Venus. This sign is about balance. They are the world's diplomats; they are cooperative, social, and fair-minded. They will always try to negotiate peace, whether between two people or two countries; this is an integral part of their nature.

Libras can give the impression of being unaware of the passage of time because it takes them quite a bit of time to come to a decision. Whether it's about what their company should do to improve service to a client or deciding on what luncheon sandwich they should order, they take their time to decide. The reason is that they need time to come to a decision that is the right one. However, when they do, it's almost always a good one, where everyone is happy in the end.

This sign likes harmony, sharing, and outdoors. They are gentle by nature. When others are happy, they're happy. When everything around them is balanced and harmonious, that's when they're the happiest.

Libras are very charming, and people are drawn to them. Any form of meditation for Libras is enjoyable because the balance that they seek is usually found in the moments of quiet and deep thought.

Libra's negative side is taking a long time to come to a decision, giving the appearance of absentmindedness or laziness. They also don't like the role of a manager or being in charge, yet they will make a point to be heard if necessary. They will argue a point if they feel a situation is unjust or unfair.

Libra is compatible with Leo, Sagittarius, Aquarius, and Gemini.

Scorpio (October 23-November 21)
The Scorpion

Scorpio, a water sign ruled by Pluto, is the eighth sign of the Zodiac. They are passionate, brave, and stubborn. They appreciate long-term friendships and are true friends.

The scorpion symbol illustrates the Scorpio persona well. This sign is not an aggressive one but will become irritated when they are prodded and aggravated. Although that provocation may move others to act, Scorpios become contemplative instead of drawn to fighting.

They are good at keeping secrets, and their emotions are felt by them more profoundly than any other sign. Scorpios' deeply felt emotions enable them to assist others with their problems. They also get to the core of any situation.

Scorpios' negative side is one you don't want to be on. The word "vendetta" is a word that some astrologers half-jokingly say Scorpio invented. Crossing them is one thing you really don't want to intentionally do because they never forget. In other words, don't get in their crosshairs.

They can also be suspicious, stubborn, and paranoid for no reason when they feel there are threats that don't really exist.

Scorpios' positive side is having enormous self-control in practically every part of their life. They are disciplined and protective. They are givers who expect to receive in return.

Scorpio is compatible with Virgo, Cancer, Pisces, and Capricorn.

Sagittarius (November 22-December 21)
The Archer

Sagittarius is a fire sign, ruled by Jupiter, and the ninth sign of the Zodiac. This sign is adventurous, creative, and happy. Those born under this sign have a love of travel, learning, and discovery of new things. They love meeting new people.

Sagittarians are generous and idealistic, and they have a good sense of humor. They don't like mundane routines or being tied down to a normal, repetitive one. Variety is their spice of life, and they become restless if there isn't enough of that.

They love to travel and search for new experiences, making them fun to be around. They have a large group of friends and socialize quite often.

The negative side of Sagittarius makes them rude and uncooperative when confined or tied down. At times, they create elaborate plans but don't follow through because they get distracted and easily sidetracked.

On the positive side, they enjoy being around people who are equally intelligent as they are. Sagittarius is also spiritually inclined and creative.

Sagittarius are compatible with Aries, Leo, Libra, and Aquarius.

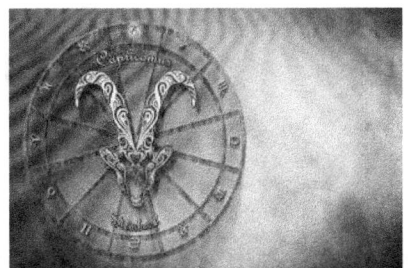

Capricorn (December 22-January 19
The Goat

Capricorn, the Earth sign ruled by Saturn, is the 10th sign of the Zodiac. The mountain goat is the symbol for Capricorn and illustrates this sign's ambition to climb higher. They are successful and goal-oriented, and they work hard to achieve their goals. They are not short-sighted, but they look at the long-term.

Their self-discipline is admirable. Some of the greatest leaders, scientists, and teachers in the world are born under Capricorn. They enjoy music and family, and they are very traditional. They love to observe the holidays with all the trimmings.

Achievement is very important to them and is serious about working toward a goal. They are intolerant of people who do not do the same.

The negative side of Capricorn is their commitment to the minutia of details and the big picture, which appears dull to others. They are always thinking, but they give the impression of being emotionless to others. They can be selfish and stingy, and they may withhold information that is valuable as a strategy for their eventual gain.

On the positive side, Capricorns can make realistic and logical decisions. They are good at seeing the bottom line, and this ability makes them an asset to any corporate position they may hold. Their humor swings between dry and sarcastic but not in a mean way. They are extremely intelligent and do well with analysis and numbers.

Capricorns are compatible with Taurus, Scorpio, Virgo, and Pisces.

Aquarius (January 20-February 18
The Water Bearer

Air sign Aquarius is the eleventh sign of the Zodiac and ruled and influenced by the outer planet of Uranus. Air signs are communicative, social, friendly, and intellectual, and they enjoy relationships. Their positive traits can be overshadowed by their penchant for being superficial.

Aquarians seem to be detached emotionally. However, when you get to really know them, you'll find they are on a much deeper plane when it comes to friendships and will find a true friend in them. If a friend or family member is feeling down, they'll be there to cheer you up.

Independence is an Aquarian's middle name and a large part of their persona. They enjoy deep relationships, but they value their independence. They love their freedom and like to have the ability to come and go whenever they want. Restricting them or tying them down will have them run in the other direction.

Aquarius can be extremely stubborn, which can occasionally interfere with their personal relationships and career. They may be shown a plethora of evidence that shows them they are wrong, but they will continue to insist on doing things their way.

However, in all their stubbornness, they do not impose their ideas on others. Aquarius has a unique quality in that they have respect for everyone's opinions and understand other people's different viewpoints and differences.

Not having their time alone is the negative side of Aquarius. They become resentful and even depressed when they don't get their space and alone time. They enjoy having time for their hobbies or extra-curricular activities, which may seem bizarre to some.

The positive side of Aquarius is they are one of the friendliest of all the other signs of the Zodiac. They acquire friends easily, and co-workers often speak highly of working with them. They are great at networking and are at ease speaking with others as though they've known each other for years. This happens with people they've just met as well. Aquarius needs time for themselves, and they do well with meditating or practicing yoga.

Aquarius is compatible with Gemini, Sagittarius, Aries, and Libra.

Pisces (February 10-March 20
The Fish

The 12th sign of the Zodiac, Pisces, was traditionally ruled by Jupiter until the discovery of Neptune and its symbol is the fish. Pisces is compassionate, wise, intuitive, and artistic. They like sleeping, solitude, music, and spiritual themes. They are also romantic.

Criticism is not something they welcome, and they abhor cruelty to people and the animal kingdom. They also dislike people who come off as know-it-alls. They frequently dwell on things that happened in the past.

Pisceans are rather easy-going and are popular with almost any kind of crowd. Their nature tends to be submissive, making them less threatening to those with whom they interact with.

This sign is selfless and helps others without any expectation of something in return. They are empathetic and emotional, faithful, caring, and compassionate. Sometimes, the troubles of others concern them more than their own.

Pisces withdraw from the real world and would rather spend time in the fantasy worlds of their making. In that world, they can be extremely wealthy. They travel the world and have a myriad of homes. They have a great appreciation for art, and they dream about traveling to exotic places.

The negative side of Pisces is how they take on the worry and problems of others. They worry themselves into illness. They don't do well in managerial positions but do excel in a support staff position.

The positive side of Pisces is their empathy for the troubles of others. They feel compassion for people who are not doing well in their lives. They are caring, and they feel deeply even if they do not show it on the surface.

Pisces is compatible with Cancer, Scorpio, Capricorn, and Taurus.

Moon Signs

Chapter 5: How to Determine Your Moon Sign

Your personality is dictated by your Sun sign, yet that is just one factor of what makes up who you are. Your emotions are part of our psychological makeup.

The Moon influences the second most significant factor of your natal chart after the Sun. It represents your emotions, moods, and how you react emotionally overall.

The Sun sign is determined by your month and day of birth. The Moon moves quickly around the Zodiac, completing its full rotation in one month, visiting all the signs. It remains in each sign for approximately two days. The time of your birth comes into play to determine your Moon sign.

If the Moon is in the process of moving to the next sign on the day of your birth, knowing the time of your birth will help you get an accurate Moon sign placement. It would be ideal to have the exact time of birth, but an approximation of the time can help an astrologer establish which sign the Moon was in at the time of your birth.

The Moon causes the high and low tides of the oceans by the gravitational pull known as the tidal force. This force causes Earth and its water to create high and low tides. In comparison, our emotions have highs and lows, causing our emotions to be amplified and our behavior affected by the moon.

Probably since the beginning of time, the moon has been linked to the changes in our behavior and mood. Studies have found a link between the number of psychiatric emergencies and the cycle of the moon.

In ancient times, the full moon was a time of much socializing activity, while a new moon would leave us in darkness, where we would go inward and reflect, remaining at home.

Today, we don't use the full moon as our light to socialize and gather, yet the innate intuitiveness continues to be wired to follow the moon cycles. Being more sociable or a bit reclusive during the new moon may be the reason for your level of activity and mood changes.

The moon's energy intensifies and heightens our emotions. Like the changing tides, a full moon can bring up all your emotions, while a new moon will be a time of reflection and calm.

So let's look at how the sign and its ruling planet affect how the Moon's emotions affect you.

If your Moon is in each of these signs, this is what you can expect about your emotional makeup.

Moon in Aries

Mars is the strong-minded planet ruling Aries. The energy can either be assertive and motivated or aggressive and determined. Mars can make you impulsive, intense, and quick to act and overreact at times. Your temper is fiery and short from this emotionally charged Moon and Mars combo.

Aries needs to be challenged and go all out on a specific level of excitement in any form. Although it is a good thing to release your bottled up energy, the person who is on the receiving end of that release may be left to feel wounded after you've moved on and forgotten about it.

Those born with the Moon in Aries have the ability from an emotional point of view not to hold any grudges. You are able to say what's on your mind, release it, forgive, and forget rather quickly.

Moon in Taurus

Venus, the love goddess and the beholder and lover of beauty, is the ruler of Taurus. This influences your inner mood. You are caring and sensitive, and well-liked. However, your caring for others can make you a target to be taken advantage of.

In love, you are a giver and expect the same in return. You have a tendency to be controlling and possessive of your partner if you suspect they may be stepping out with another. You become hurt if you are disrespected or if your desires are not met.

You are open and loving if you are treated well, the best friend or lover. Your surroundings affect you, and you do cope with life better if your surroundings are comfortable and secure.

Moon in Gemini

Gemini is ruled by the planet of communication, Mercury. If there isn't enough activity to give you mental stimulation, you will become bored easily. This leaves time to play tricks and be mischievous. You don't mean any harm; it's just for fun.

The challenge to a Moon in Gemini is slowing down and not to have an activity to be part of constantly. You can stop and reflect on how you feel rather than how you *think*.

However, that is not so simple for a Gemini or a Gemini Moon. When your emotions are confronted, you would rather look at things how you want them to be instead of how they really are.

You are curious, clever, and have a playfulness about you. You can be open-hearted and sentimental when you let your feelings show.

Moon in Cancer

The Moon rules Cancer, and the pairing with this sign makes you incredibly emotional and sensitive. With the quick change of signs the Moon makes, this consistent change can make you moodier than most.

You will rarely go against the way you feel, even if something appears to be reasonably sound. You will operate by your feelings and make decisions based on intuition and impulse.

Your feelings are hurt rather easily, but that outer shell of protection from your symbol, the crab, will have you protect yourself by pulling back and shutting down. You have strength, emotionally, that may appear fragile but is actually pretty resolute.

You give people an ample amount of warnings and chances, and if they continue to provoke you or tinker with your heart and emotions, you have been known to cut all ties without a backward glance. The door is locked once you decide to close the door. When treated well, you are a protective, nurturing, and loyal friend or partner.

Moon in Leo

The center of our solar system, the Sun, the most powerful of forces and ruler of Leo, gives you the ability to have the resilience and confidence to take charge of your emotions, as well as your life.

You endeavor to be a leader, and when your talents are admired and recognized, you excel. You do tend to be bossy when your emotions are out of sorts, along with your conceited and petty attitude.

You are generous of the spirit and heart, extravagant, and exuberant. You care deeply for those who give you love and support. Your pride and emotions are connected, and since you love being the center of attention, you have high emotions when you are in the front and center, proud of what you do and who you are.

Moon in Virgo

You are an intelligent being if your Moon is in the sign of Virgo, ruled by Mercury. You have a strong sense of self and are emotionally reserved.

Your tendency to get caught up in the minutia of details and over-analysis distracts you from how you feel emotionally and the big picture in general.

You tend to be picky and critical. This is the way Virgos are but with only those people you care about and love. Anyone else wouldn't even be a blip on your caring radar. You will reach out and offer your care and advice to only those who appreciate the effort, which is when you are at your emotional best.

The person you are most critical of is yourself. You critique yourself the hardest because you strive for an outcome that is frequently unattainable. You need to be kind to yourself, which is the best solution to your criticizing yourself.

Moon in Libra

Libra is ruled by Venus, the planet of grace, beauty, and love. These are all the things a Libra must have. Libra is the sign of balance and the sign of the scales. Your emotions are balanced by keeping the people you interact with. You also keep your environment balanced. You like to keep it all as harmonious as possible.

You sometimes put others' needs before yours and keep everything and everyone agreeable because you look to get along with people. That may be a good thing for other people, but your balance is upset and unsettled if you're in disagreement with others.

You may give up too much of your needs and go too far in the direction of pleasing others and feel you've been taken advantage of and become irritable.

Look for the balance between others' needs and your needs—that is the balance you will need.

Moon in Scorpio

Pluto, the planet of transformation, is Scorpio's ruler. Pluto influences the inner world of those with their Moon in Scorpio with power, intensity, and the desire to look deep for the truth. Honest connections with others include passionate, sensitive, and strong expression that brings emotional fulfillment.

When you are angry or upset, you'll never let on to others because you hide your emotions under a glacial demeanor that does not reveal your disposition. This is your secret weapon, and others may become suspicious.

You live for emotional intensity and the drama of life because it gives you the feeling of being alive. However, when you have a tight rein and control over your own emotions, you feel the most powerful.

You have an intense emotional commitment with those you care for, and you surround them with protectiveness and love that is incomparable by any other.

Moon in Sagittarius

Jupiter, the planet of expansion and wisdom, is the ruler of Sagittarius. Your emotions are high with the desire to explore the world of different beliefs. You have a thirst for knowledge, and you have the spirit of adventure.

You are a truth seeker and feel unsettled if you are obliged to keep a secret rather than tell others quite bluntly what they need to know. You are of the mind that even if the truth hurts, it will allow you to feel satisfied and relieve the emotional tension.

Living life to the fullest is how you want to experience life and prefer that someone is beside you, enjoying it with you, even if a commitment is something you shy away from.

By nature, you are optimistic and positive, and you won't remain in a negative mood for long. Your outlook on life is forward-looking, and that's how you like it.

Moon in Capricorn

The planet of reality and ruler of Capricorn, serious Saturn, the planet of reality and the teacher, will infuse your mood with a driven, solitary, and no-nonsense quality.

In order to keep your emotions balanced, there is a time between the busy schedule you keep and getting together with others in the social world. You need time to decompress. But it is important not to remain in solitude for too long; you need time to avert a down-in-the-dumps blues.

You do well when mixing with others, but you can be at ease with your own company. You need to feel that you have a feeling of worth in this world. In your later years, when you have a sense of achievement, you can feel settled and relaxed. Your heart is not something you give easily to another, but when you find someone special to trust and love, you give them your all.

Moon in Aquarius

Uranus, the planet of innovation and independence, is the ruler of Aquarius. This planet infuses your mood with your refusal to walk in another's shoes and individuality that separates you from the rest.

A groundbreaker, you can be in your own world, giving the impression that you are standoffish when, in reality, you are categorizing things in your mind. People who are secure within their own selves do better in associating with someone whose Moon is in Aquarius.

If your Moon is in Aquarius, you need your freedom to be who you are, and you need to be with those who understand this about you and not take your "distancing" personally. Only then can your emotional balance be achieved; otherwise, you will have to deal with someone else's anxieties.

You and your emotions can be unpredictable. To soothe your soul and your emotions, having an extensive conversation with someone will do you well.

Moon in Pisces

Neptune, the planet of compassion and inspiration, is the ruler of Pisces and influences your emotions with deep empathy and sensitivity. Meditative silence allows you to gain access to your imagination and dreams, make a spiritual connection, and keep your emotions controlled. What helps you to be effective in the world is a balance between reality and escapism—to have a place to claim as a sanctuary, an escape where you feel comfortable. Safety is a major factor in your happiness.

Those with their Moon in Pisces are highly sensitive and show the feelings of their emotional state. For this reason, and because there is an innocence about you, there is a need for you to be careful of the people you select and allow to share your life with. You have a tendency to take on other people's emotions and attitudes because you care too much.

The symbol of the two fishes is a sign of duality, and in order to maintain emotional stability in your life, you need to have a balance between your mind and your heart. You will feel at peace with yourself if you follow this guideline.

Your Sun Sign ↓	Your Hour of Birth											
	6am to 8am	8am to 10am	10am to 12pm	12pm to 2pm	2pm to 4pm	4pm to 6pm	6pm to 8pm	8pm to 10pm	10pm to 12am	12am to 2am	2am to 4am	4am to 6am
Aries ♈	♉	♊	♋	♌	♍	♎	♏	♐	♑	♒	♓	♈
Taurus ♉	♊	♋	♌	♍	♎	♏	♐	♑	♒	♓	♈	♉
Gemini ♊	♋	♌	♍	♎	♏	♐	♑	♒	♓	♈	♉	♊
Cancer ♋	♌	♍	♎	♏	♐	♑	♒	♓	♈	♉	♊	♋
Leo ♌	♍	♎	♏	♐	♑	♒	♓	♈	♉	♊	♋	♌
Virgo ♍	♎	♏	♐	♑	♒	♓	♈	♉	♊	♋	♌	♍
Libra ♎	♏	♐	♑	♒	♓	♈	♉	♊	♋	♌	♍	♎
Scorpio ♏	♐	♑	♒	♓	♈	♉	♊	♋	♌	♍	♎	♏
Sagittarius ♐	♑	♒	♓	♈	♉	♊	♋	♌	♍	♎	♏	♐
Capricorn ♑	♒	♓	♈	♉	♊	♋	♌	♍	♎	♏	♐	♑
Aquarius ♒	♓	♈	♉	♊	♋	♌	♍	♎	♏	♐	♑	♒
Pisces ♓	♈	♉	♊	♋	♌	♍	♎	♏	♐	♑	♒	♓

Your Rising Sign

Chapter 6: Your Rising Sign

The third element of your astrological chart that determines the development of a person's character and how it influences their physical characteristics is your Ascendant, also known as your Rising sign.

How others see you is what your Ascendant represents. In your first meeting with someone, you will most likely be meeting their rising sign. Those who know very little about astrology could be surprised how much influence their ascendant applies to their character.

The ascendant is a significant part of your natal chart and is based on the sign and degree that was on the horizon right at the time of your birth. For example, if the sign of Leo was at the 9 o'clock position on the horizontal line of your astrological chart, it is your Ascendant.

The way to locate your ascendant to apply it to your natal chart is to have the date of your birth and the time and place of your birth. Every two hours, the ascendant changes, which is why you should try to have the most accurate information possible about the time of your birth.

The rising sign has an importance of its own, separate from your Sun sign. The twelve astrological houses are set in their positions from the rising sign.

The only way for your Sun sign and Ascendant to be the same is if you were born at dawn. So, for example, if you were both Sun in Scorpio and Scorpio rising, it would be known as a double Scorpio.

Aries Ascendant

Aries ascendants are quick and direct. They usually do rather than think. They never plan ahead. They simply begin doing whatever it is without much forethought and get it done.

A person with an Aries ascendant is not aggressive, as much as they are candid in what they say. Their manner is direct and youthful, and when they see what they want, they usually go after it. However, there's no intent of malice in their actions.

There are some Aries rising individuals who are competitive, but the pressure is usually on themselves. They strive to come out on top in all things they do. They are quick in every action they take—walking, getting dressed—and they have little time or patience in dawdling.

They're quick in the temper department as well, but that is quick to disappear and move on as well. Aries rising people rarely hold grudges.

People with Aries rising sign love action and lots of activity. Sometimes, completing things that they had begun doesn't come easily.

Aries Ascendants have a quick walk with their head leaning slightly forward, like the ram. They complain of sinus irritation, eye problems, and headaches. Acne and rashes on their faces and upper body are also maladies they may have.

Aries rising people are self-reliant, and this is generally learned from their early childhood experiences. They are usually willing to compromise in relationships, and they are very close to those whom they care for.

Taurus Ascendant

Taurus rising is slow, capable, and steady. This is how to describe those born with a Taurus Ascendant. Their stamina and fortitude are tremendous. They are very loyal to the people they care about. They radiate stability and exhibit personal presence yet, generally, do not come on strong.

Generally, the sign on the Ascendant discloses how people begin new things. By nature, Taurus usually resists change, and it can be a bit difficult to persuade those with Taurus rising sign since this sign is frequently fixed in their ways. They usually respond by feeling things out before they act. Their security is their most important considerations before they decide to engage in anything new.

These Taurus rising natives are careful and cautious and are not known for being flexible, considering the ascendant's fixed sign. They are single-minded in their thinking.

Taurus rising sign enjoys the luxury and good things in life. Their weakness can be self-indulgence, and they place quite a bit of value on their material items.

Taurus rising individuals have physiques that are solid and strong. They rarely dress flashy or showy, and they usually like quality clothing and dress for comfort.

These Taurus rising natives don't break up their relationships easily and are somewhat possessive in their partnerships. They don't display jealously yet view their partners as personal property. They consider loyalty to be extremely important.

Taurus rising individuals are very sensual and prefer the stability of one-on-one partnerships, and although they enjoy calm and harmony, their partnerships may be passionate.

These Taurus rising natives have stability about them that is soothing and inner peace that is comforting to be around.

Gemini Ascendant

People born with Gemini rising sign look at the world as a place to learn. They are interested and curious about those around them. They love to freely move around, ask questions, and mingle with others.

They have a restless streak and are quick in their physical expression. Gemini rising sign gives off an air of impatience even if it's not meant. There is wittiness to Gemini Ascendants that sometimes can intimidate those who are more sensitive.

People with Gemini rising sign has an aptitude with words, which can be a great asset. However, these individuals identify a bit too much with their cleverness. They forget their personal communications with others to nurture and cultivate those around them. Although a lack of warmth in the way they present themselves is generally a façade, it is not immediately clear to most that a Gemini is hiding behind a mask.

There are two descriptions of the presentation that is common with Gemini Ascendants. One is changeable, talkative, and a bit quirky. They are fun and interesting. They explain and clarify things, whether it's an opinion, the world, or even their own behavior.

The other description is an intellectual with a cool attitude and who is clever and witty but not as changeable and animated or cheerful as the other group. They have sharp views, and their manner can be abrupt.

Regardless of which style they are, Gemini rising individuals are analytical. Their observations are progressive, and they are mentally active. At times, they are easily sidetracked because they have a large capacity for curiosity. Their minds are quick, while their attention span can be short.

Gemini rising individuals frequently look for a particular amount of space and freedom for their personal self. These Gemini Ascendants enjoy intellectual debates and the exchange of ideas and ideals.

A Gemini always welcomes some freedom and is willing to give breathing room and space to their partners.

Cancer Ascendant

Cancer rising people give the appearance of being gentle. When they enter a room, they don't burst into it. Instead, they move to the sides of the room and work their way to the center. They get flustered, particularly in public, and are sensitive to their environment.

When they are on an unfamiliar ground or feel threatened, their first instinct is to be self-protective, withdrawing shyly when new situations arise. On the whole,

Cancer rising people appear to be caring, sweet, and even innocent. They seem unassuming enough to be approachable. However, there are those Cancer Ascendants who have withdrawn so much to become not as approachable as it might seem.

Cancer rising people look for security and structure in a relationship and partner. These individuals are at their best when they have a partner who exhibits financial and emotional stability, strength, and capability.

Many Cancer Ascendants like it when there are defined rules and structure in their relationship. Their security is a need that Cancer ascendants have, and they will give up some of their personal freedom in order to have that security.

Cancer rising people appear to be quiet and family-oriented, but they have a pragmatic approach to marriage.

Cancer rising people appear to be quiet and family-oriented yet have a pragmatic approach to marriage.

Leo Ascendant

Leo rising people get noticed without trying. They radiate a magnetism and energy that draw the attention of others. Sometimes, it's because they can be loud, giving attention to their appearance. At other times, it's their regal manner that gets the attention and interest of others.

Leo Ascendants are self-aware of themselves, including their physical appearance. They consider how others appear, and they are aware of the people they are with, the surroundings they are in, and what it does to their own image. Leo rising people think they're on a stage, even in their own homes.

They have a natural optimism and enthusiasm about beginning anything new, and sometimes, they overestimate things, including themselves. Leo rising people are good promoters, and they can be walking commercials.

Leo Ascendants pay attention to their mannerisms and appearance and have a strong physical structure. They usually like hairstyles and clothing that are youthful, while their manner is strong and autocratic.

Regardless of their age, people with Leo rising signs are generous and spirited, warm, and love to have fun. Basically, they are kids at heart.

Leo rising individuals, and how selfless they are, will be altered by which sign and house the Sun is in at the time of their birth. This is because the Sun is the ruler of a Leo Ascendant. Regardless of the placement of the Sun, Leo rising people are optimistic and self-aware. They always want to create a stir when they can.

Virgo Ascendant

Virgo rising natives frequently downplay their appearance and mannerisms, although it depends on where Mercury, Virgo's ruling planet, was positioned in the astrological chart at the time of their birth.

Virgo rising people have reserved aura and intelligence that is distinct. Actually, they are a bit shy and need time before they can warm up to people and situations to analyze them. Their analytical nature can be accepted for what it is, or it can be seen as cool, critical, and, in a manner, standoffish.

Body awareness is Virgo rising sign's biggest personality attribute. Virgo ascendants are conscious of any signals of discomfort that their body gives them. They are particularly concerned with their physical health, and some Virgo rising natives are interested in mind-body awareness and engage in exercises like yoga.

Although they have good appetites, Virgo ascendants are picky about their food and what they ingest into their bodies.

These Virgo rising natives tend to worry, particularly when encountering new situations. There are details that others overlook that a Virgo rising will notice down to the tiniest one.

Virgo rising natives attract or are attracted to people in need. Because of this, their relationships may be complex. Virgo's tendency is to appear professional and coolly possessed, yet their relationships can become disorderly and muddled because these natives do not see clearly when it comes to their partnerships and partners.

Virgo rising natives possess a quiet charm. Once given the opportunity to warm up to new situations and people, one can discover that they have quite a bit to offer. They'll be helpful to you when there's a problem or issue; they will stick their neck out for you, and you'll be amazed at their modesty hidden under that aloof and critical manner.

Libra Ascendant

Libra Ascendants appears to be liked by everyone. They present themselves as pleasant, nice, and fair, but if you look a bit closer, they seem to have a few problems in their relationships.

These Libra rising natives attract others to them without even trying, and some have a string of relationships. They just don't know what to do without having a significant other.

Libra rising have a gentle approach with everyone, a charming smile, an even-tempered image, and they generally appear to be able to smooth everything over. Most of these Libra Ascendants pay quite a bit of attention to their personal appearance—what they wear, the color, the way they walk, and their hair. Even if they were not blessed with good looks, they're attractive to others.

Libra rising natives usually use a soft sell approach when trying to win others over (which is usually all the time, and they can be extremely, extremely persuasive. Their worst quality is maintaining their nice person image by passing the responsibility in a situation or issue on to someone else. However, they do make good mediators and will be the first to help you.

Libra rising natives are attracted to active, competent partners. Their relationships often have competitiveness or bickering in the mix until they realize they have to drop the nice person image every now and again, and they need to end the "blaming their partner game" for everything that goes wrong.

Scorpio Ascendant

Scorpio rising has quite a bit of presence. There is an aura about them that gives notice to the world that they won't be pushed around. Their demeanor commands respect and fear, in some cases. Quiet or loud, Scorpio rising people always seem to be determined and powerful.

Whether you love or hate Scorpio rising natives, they very rarely go through life unnoticed. When faced with the idea, they get strong reactions from others; they are somewhat bewildered.

Their ability to see right through people and their façade can be intriguing to some and intimidating to others. When Scorpio rising people deal with others, they usually look for answers by reading between the lines. They get rid of surface details when they get a feel for the situations and people around them.

Scorpio rising natives need to control their environment and value their privacy to the point that borders on paranoia. They plan their moves rather deliberately and rely on their capability to examine situations and others.

Scorpio rising people are attracted to natural, commonsensical partners. They value reliability in their partners and, in general, don't waste their time on flighty partners. They look for partners that can give them a complete commitment.

Sagittarius Ascendant

This rising sign represents new things to encounter, a world filled with adventure and hope. Enthusiasm and faith are unmistakable with Sagittarius rising people. The enjoyment of exploring, big promises, and grand schemes are its themes. However, a not-so-strong characteristic of Sagittarius is follow-through.

Restless and frequently active, Sagittarius rising natives always seem to be seeking something that's just out of reach. Many do this over their lifetime. They can be direct at times to a fault but are appealing enough to be forgiven. They have lots to offer, and their observations and opinions are usually interesting, although they sometimes don't provide enough details.

Sagittarius rising people like to tell others exactly what they are, and they have opinions about everything. Some people in this position have a way of radiating a certain level of confidence, and some may even call them overly optimistic or even naïve. Even the quiet Sagittarians don't shy away from experience and life.

Sagittarius rising natives are always willing to keep a sense of humor, which is an endearing characteristic. They manage humor in life and have fun, even when they're feeling low.

Capricorn Ascendant

There is an unmistakable seriousness to Capricorn rising natives. Even when they're kidding around, they do so in a deadpan way. Actually, there are quite a few humorous people who have Capricorn Ascendants. In fact, they have great timing, and they don't giggle before the joke is over.

Competence is the word that comes to mind when you think of Capricorn Ascendant people. They exude it. They are image-conscious and are very particular about the clothes they wear, and their way of presenting themselves to the world is a big deal to them. They want to present that they are successful.

In childhood, Capricorn Ascendants were the children who were considered the conscientious and responsible ones. Sometimes, they look around themselves and feel there is a need to be the dependable, capable, and structured members of their family. Capricorn rising natives take on the responsibility of their family at a young age.

Capricorn rising people are forever concerned about being secure for their dependents and themselves. Underneath the hard-working, dependable character with a cool exterior that they convey to the world is someone who is enmeshed in an inner struggle. They continually ask themselves if they're doing enough or if they deserve all that they have worked for, and they worry about the future.

If you look at Capricorn Ascendants and think their success has come easy, believe that it has not. They make it look easy, but they are hard-working, driven, and patient to get where they're going. Some Capricorn rising people do away with frivolous spending. However, they'll spend money on clothing that bears the right labels and those they really want and other status-symbol items. Showiness for them is rare, and their success is a result of conscious effort.

Capricorn rising people are, more often than not, people who become successful. They may have had difficult childhoods, but they have the ability to turn their lives around to achieve the success they want it to be.

Aquarius Ascendant

Aquarius rising natives can be described as original, unique, and just plain different, and they won't let you forget it. Aquarius rising people have savvy and intellectual aplomb and are often sought out for their advice. For these natives, there is an appeal for both metaphysics and science and an interest in advancing the human race.

The people with this sign are not easily shocked—they have seen or done it all or may want you to think they have. They sometimes get a kick in shocking others. They're not flashy or gaudy by nature, but getting a rise out of others gives them a special glee. Some Aquarius on their Ascendant can be irreverent and provocative, albeit quietly.

Aquarian rising people are likable and friendly, and the quirks in their personalities are relatively accepted by others. They themselves give others freedom, and they view equality in people from all backgrounds. Their somewhat detached and cool curiosity about everything around them, whether it's the environment or the people, appeals to others.

They are humanitarians and kind, but they can come across as somewhat standoffish. Some devote their humanitarianism to animals and children, and it isn't a surprise to find they contribute money and time to those causes.

Aquarius Ascendants feel special or different throughout their lives and have been labeled as original and independent as children. Some feel they exist on the "outside looking in," and their ability to surmise by observing is frequently uncanny.

They have the ability to get things to work, piecing together the whole with unusual ones that don't seem to fit but do, in the end. This works for them, particularly when it comes to groups of people, and it makes them good team leaders and managers.

Aquarius rising natives sometimes have an eccentricity to their manner, and some have an offbeat way of dressing. It may not be dressing to look or stand out like a sore thumb but enough to let them express their originality. Their choice of clothes shows how they present themselves to the world.

There is definitely a stubborn streak in these Aquarius rising people, which may surprise some who see this sign as open to new ideas. Aquarius is a fixed sign, and with Aquarius, there are those who will be resistant to change. This characteristic seems to contradict their generally forward-looking nature. There's a tendency to try and force their own opinions on others, and there's inflexibility with Aquarius rising natives.

Some Aquarius Ascendants, at times, ignore the needs of the people closest to them and are frequently attracted to those who possess passion and self-confidence.

Pisces Ascendant

Pisces rising has a motto that almost everyone, at one time or the other, has thought or said—go with the flow. They have a gentle yet directionless manner. They move like this throughout the world. This description somewhat describes how a fish move through the water, gentle and directionless.

Pisces rising people have open hearts and minds and appear to others as artists and peace lovers. Yet, they seem to have a chameleon-like persona. One is not quite sure which persona you'll have to interact with each time. One day, they may be passionate and talkative with everyone, and the next day, they will be shy and quiet.

Pisces Ascendants are impressionable, are soft-hearted, and can come across as dreamy. They're not objective and see the world in the way that they want to view it. They're not very objective when making decisions as well.

Pisces rising natives don't like to be labeled as any one thing. They don't want to be pinned or pegged in any way, as their characters are changeable. They are not happy living in any one way due to their restless nature that is constantly searching and changing. They don't have a plan that's solid or decisive for tomorrow or, for that matter, even today. They prefer to keep all options open. Structure and organization for them are rather limiting because, in their changing of their minds or what they want to do at any given time, they like to feel their way through life.

If you don't own a fish tank, go to an aquarium and watch how the fish glide in and out of all the caves and sea plants, heading one way one minute and then another way. This will give you an idea as to what goes on in a Pisces rising native's mind and way of being.

These people look for partnerships that are reliable and stable. Pisces rising natives are inclined to seek partners who are challenging. There seems to be a need for a realistic, practical partner.

Pisces Ascendants are sometimes prone to allergies and frequently have a drug sensitivity. Their physical constitution and the immune system seem to be less resistant than most.

Pisces rising natives are often blessed with a charm that's irresistible and a soft aura surrounding them. This charm isn't a loud, center-of-attention charm but one that is quiet in its own way. They intrigue others with their mannerisms and appearance.

Cusp Signs

Chapter 7: Are You Born on a Cusp?

When someone asks the question, "what's your sign?" they'll probably give you the one-word answer of Aquarius or Scorpio (although this Sun sign likes to be mysterious about it, so you may not get an answer), or Leo because we all know they are ruled by the Sun, the center of everything, pretty much Leo's personality.

But what about those individuals who were born on a cusp, i.e., being born under two signs? What about the duality of it all—that gray area when the Sun transitions out of one sign into the next one? Those born on the cusp may feel they have an identity dilemma and are affected by two different signs, which can sometimes be quite the opposite of one another.

Is it possible that a person born on the cusp is likely to retain the traits of both signs, even though they can only identify with one Sun sign?

The zone that identifies the cusp of each astrological sign is determined by the five days that surround the date that the sun officially transitions into the next sign.

For example, if you were born between April 19 and April 23, you are born on the cusp of Aries the Ram and Taurus the Bull. This can bring a fiery go-getter, quick quality of Aries to the otherwise slow, plodding of Taurus.

Even if you were born on the transitional day of two signs, such as October 24 when Libra moves into Scorpio, the person born on this day is either a Libra or, without a doubt, a Scorpio, so there's no reason to have to read two horoscopes like you do if you're reading not only your Sun sign but your Ascendant sign as well. It is helpful to check out both signs because it can be helpful if you're confused about the birth sign you identify with.

The birth on a cusp is complex, and each cusp is like a sign on its own, with the original 12 astrological signs becoming 24 in all. (Cafe Astrology staff, 2019)

Each of the following cusps is a guide of how a sign's planet and element affects the other.

Aries-Taurus Cusp (April 17–23) — The Cusp of Power

This cusp characterizes the natural leadership of Aries and the details from the disciplinarian Taurus, and don't forget how much quicker Taurus will move with the quickness of the Aries sign's influence.

Both the active Mars and the sensual lover of beauty, Venus, the planets that rule Aries and Taurus, influence those born on this cusp.

Mars is the planet of drive and motivation, while Venus epitomizes beauty and persuasion. This energy combination is a blend that is unstoppable on the way up to the goal of success.

Aries' element of Fire and the Taurean element of Earth mix together on this cusp to give you a personality that is brave yet grounded. There is the energy to advance in situations or projects and steadiness to see things through to completion. Remember to consider the project before you act so you don't get stuck in something, and you won't quit because of your stubbornness.

You know how to have fun and a good time while you make your way to the top if you're born on the Cusp of Power. You have outgoing social skills that can get you anywhere you wish. You can handle quite a bit; your thick skin helps with that. Your independence can sometimes detach you from those who love you. Don't let that happen because you do need them. Have patience. Realize that leaders who are kind can accomplish great things.

Strengths – Fun, smart, energetic, humorous, brave

Weaknesses – Self-centered, controlling, pushy, stubborn, insensitive

Taurus-Gemini Cusp (May 17–23) — The Cusp of Energy

Those born on the Taurus-Gemini cusp give you the dual bonus of having the physical strength and mental agility. This cusp is a social, youthful spirit.

The impact of the sensual, friendly Venus, ruler of Taurus, and the sociable and quick Mercury, ruler of Gemini, makes you rather the socialite. This mix of energy gives you the ability to easily make friends, as well as sustain great relationships. You love to talk; you are very clever, witty, and loving, which are qualities that make you very popular with all sorts of people.

The Taurean Earth sign, meeting the Gemini Air sign on the Cusp of Energy, creates quite a storm of activity. You have the ability to be both flexible and stable, depending on the situation. You are able to be adaptable and enjoy wherever you are. You have the endurance to accomplish all you want to and then do more if you want.

You are able to converse easily, and social settings are just the thing you like after a day of accomplishing your goals. It doesn't matter whether you're meeting someone new or catching up with a long-time friend; you are always fun and have something interesting to say. You love to have a fun night out, meeting friends at the newest restaurant in town. Something, like enjoying a concert or having a hot date with your partner, is what you feel life is all about. You burn the candle at both ends at times, and sometimes, it could get the better of you.

You're not unbeatable, and while it's true you're a fireball of energy, you tend to overdo it in drink and food, spending, physical activity, and not making time to get enough rest. Beware of the toll that the never-ending party can take on you, your health, and your finances. Enjoy yourself, but be smart and careful in what you do.

Your energy and exciting nature inspire others, and your smooth-talking is persuasive. There are those who may resist but others who you convince to do what you ask of them.

Allow others to have the spotlight every now and then. You're sometimes so busy socializing and chatting that you forget to share the limelight. You are charismatic, so much so that there are those who would love to have that ability. Make sure that you use your charisma with poise and dignity. You'll build fulfilling friendships for a lifetime.

Strengths – Fun, adaptable, amusing, charming, energetic, sociable

Weaknesses – Reckless, impatient, self-absorbed, wild, lenient, brash

Gemini-Cancer Cusp (June 18–24) — The Cusp of Magic

A kind, fanciful, and fun person with a gigantic heart is born on the Gemini-Cancer cusp, the Cusp of Magic. Your childlike and loving manner will afford you a continuously happy life.

Quick and curious Mercury, the planet ruling of Gemini, and the emotional Moon, the planet ruling Cancer, are a combination of energies that make you sociable and enable you to have durable relationships. Your interest in others is sincere, and you really want to know how someone feels when you ask them how they are.

The Air sign, Gemini's element, fills you with curiosity, and the Water sign, Cancer's element, gives you a sense of sentimentality. Air and Water can combine and be fun, but they can also overwhelm you. You have sensitivity and empathy, but they can overflow if you aren't logical and you don't keep things in perspective. Balancing these energies will help you to be a perceptive and emotionally intelligent friend for your partner, family, and friends.

Communication is a gift that comes from being born on the Cusp of Magic because you are a good listener and communicator. Sharing witty and interesting stories, or being a sounding board for a loved one who needs some advice, you handle yourself elegantly with any group. People confide in you, and, although you are a dedicated conversationalist, you have difficulty sharing your feelings with others. It doesn't come as easily as others who share their feelings with you.

You appear to be easy and carefree on the exterior, but your inner self may be a wound-up ball of tension. You're very sensitive, and you soak up the emotions and feelings of others. You lack trust in people and urge people to talk about themselves or interact with others in relaxed conversation to evade talking about yourself and your own issues. Having a partner will help you handle your problems rather than attempt to handle them alone.

You are cared for, and the people around you are extremely supportive. Don't fear to talk about your own issues. It's the emotional balance you need to live a contented and happy life.

Strengths – Flirty, fun, affectionate, intellectual, curious, dedicated, sensitive, inspiring

Weaknesses – Emotional, moody, depressive, flighty, self-absorbed, self-destructive

Cancer-Leo Cusp (July 19–25) — The Cusp of Oscillation

Let's begin with the word oscillation. According to Merriam-Webster, the meaning is a fluctuation between beliefs, opinions, and conditions. Now that there's clarity about the definition, it somewhat explains the Cancer-Leo cusp.

Those born on the Cancer-Leo cusp have a vast range of personality characteristics that will make or break these individuals. Born on the Cusp of Oscillations, this makes for a very influential and powerful person.

These two very different zodiac signs—Cancer ruled by the emotional, sensitive Moon, and Leo, the brave and proud sign ruled by the impassioned Sun—can be affected by both the Moon and the Sun, which can be advantageous but challenging as well. Learning to fluctuate between these two energies, you'll be able to feel and understand your emotions, as well as the emotions of others. You'll learn how to articulate and act on them applicably.

People born on this cusp have two very different elements of Cancer's Water and Leo's Fire. This combination can create scorching steam! Your mood may switch from a melodramatic queen to a sensitive and shy individual. The element of Water underlines your emotions, yet Fire can bring on these unpredictable moments. Taking action with your feelings is fine, as long as they're channeled into love and not hostility or self-protectiveness.

You're a leader and a lover when born on the Cusp of Oscillation, helping you to be both persuasive and powerful. You have an honest interest and empathy for others, which gives you the ability to bond with people easily. You can be ready to lead once you've won their trust.

You are a wonderful combination of being passionate and caring, and you can use the energy to assist others in need or bring awareness to good causes. Your emotional perception and charisma give you the capability of motivating people and having them do as you ask. Be careful to use this for good and not your personal gain.

You'll find that you easily influence people. When the Sun and Moon planets are balanced and in sync, you'll do incredible things that help others and for the greater good. But, if the energies are out of sync, and the Moon sensitivity or the dramatic Sun are overpowering you, you may be motivated to manipulate the situation or others.

Those born on the Cancer-Leo cusp have the ability to be a versatile, effective individual. Two vastly different signs are your influence, and it will take a bit of work on your part to keep these two energies balanced and in sync, instead of against one another.

When you merge your confidence in yourself with your empathy and care for others, you can become a deeply respected, successful leader. It is fulfilling to devote your time to assisting others and creating a positive difference. Balance these two signs and their elements, and you will accomplish incredible things.

Strengths – Dedicated, creative, loving, passionate, sensitive

Weaknesses – Overly sensitive, melodramatic, volatile, self-absorbed, dependent

Leo-Virgo Cusp (August 19–25) — The Cusp of Exposure

You have a vision for the world, you are a natural leader, and you can command a room if you are born on the Leo-Virgo Cusp. Born on the Cusp of Exposure, with your balance in sync, your destiny is to be a success.

Born on this Cusp, the Sun, Leo's ruling planet, and Mercury, Virgo's ruling planet, influence your characteristics of being big and bright. You are able to think, process, and speak about all the tiny details. Both these elements are strong forces that have you both thinking intensely and acting in a big way. Balancing these two elements is important to find harmony.

These two elements, the passion and intensity of the Fire sign of Leo and the durability of the Earth sign of Virgo, can be extremely complex to blend. The good news is that you can charm anyone. You have a childlike charisma in nature, and you are loyal to those you trust.

You have lofty standards, and it's a wonder that anyone meets or exceeds your expectations. However, those who do are compensated by your appreciation and praise, making you a great leader, as long as you stay modest and gracious in the success you achieve.

Although your impressive energy may be inspiring to some, being born on the Cusp of Exposure has you running the risk of becoming bossy and domineering. There is a delicate balance that needs to be maintained between these two elements. You're very smart, yet it's up to you to remain humble and diplomatic about it. Don't show off your braininess and go around making corrections of others' work. You may lose the respect you've worked hard to achieve.

You see the goals and the big picture and have the ability to reduce them down to the smallest of details, delineating which steps need to be taken to reach those goals. You can be smart and charming or rude, loud, and bossy. The balance of this cusp needs to happen, not to lean too far on one side or the other.

Maintain a healthy balance, and be the humble, gentle, and motivated person that you can be to achieve your goals.

Strengths – Passionate, loyal, honest, hardworking, responsible, successful

Weaknesses – Stubborn, argumentative, critical, controlling, manipulative, brusque

Virgo-Libra Cusp (September 19–25) — The Cusp of Beauty

Beautiful inside and out is the person born on the Virgo-Libra Cusp. Born on the Cusp of Beauty, you are balanced, graceful, and a vision of perfection.

People born on the Virgo-Libra Cusp are influenced by Virgo's ruling planet, Mercury, and Libra's ruling planet of Venus. They have charm and wit. This combination can make you incredibly persuasive if you use it correctly.

The Earth sign of Virgo gives you grounded determination, and the social charisma and ease of the Air sign Libra make this mix of elements a blissful, happy one. Your understanding of the world is realistic, and you share your thoughts articulately and fairly. You are extremely well-liked.

You are generous and elegant, and, no matter how you look, you're an air of loveliness. You're beloved by family and friends, as well as all those who have the chance to be enchanted by your gentle heart and kind words. You abhor cruelty and admire all those who fight for equality.

Although you usually are calm and cool, you easily get upset when your standards are not met by others, and the bar is set pretty high. If someone tells a joke that is crass or vulgar, they will hear your disdain rather quickly. You cringe at that type of behavior. However, be careful not to stick your nose up too high. People are prone to mistakes and need to have the opportunity to be human. No one is perfect. Loosening your perfectionist attitudes and learning to breathe will make others inspired by your example.

Strengths – Intelligent, attractive, communicative, artistic, sensuous, social

Weaknesses – Materialistic, detached, perfectionist, superficial, jaded

Libra-Scorpio Cusp (October 19–25) — The Cusp of Drama

People born under this cusp draw people in and spew them out just as fast. This is the persona of those born on the Cusp of Drama and Criticism, and you excel at both.

You're influenced by two appealing and commanding planets Libra's ruling planet of Venus, the planet of beauty and love, and Scorpio's ruling planet of Pluto, the dark and mysterious planet renowned for its passion and depth. Individuals born on this cusp are magnetic and, whether you know it or not, has the ability of seduction.

Libra's Air element and Scorpio's Water element meet on the Cusp of Drama and Criticism, and they can be cool and calm or a dangerous storm. Whether you are an extrovert or an introvert, you have a storm rumbling internally in your heart and head. Total honesty and truth are the only things that give you a feeling of being settled.

People appreciate your frankness even if they seem daunted by you. There is rarely a gray area with you—right and wrong are black and white, and you don't hesitate to voice your opinion when something is unjust. You're intelligent and watchful, so you see things rather quickly while it may take others a while to catch on. Have some patience when articulating your judgment; you may drive everyone away otherwise.

You abhor liars and dishonesty, and it's hard to allow others in because of your mistrust of people. You still desire relationships because of your emotional makeup. Don't be afraid to let people in. You just need to trust your intuition about others.

People born on this cusp have magnetism and charm that essentially give you control over any situation. You will go deep to learn the truth and get reasonable results. You are judgmental due to your ability to see right from wrong. Learn to be more open-minded to have true relationships and lead a satisfying life.

Strengths – Competent, powerful, charming, intelligent, honest, provocative

Weaknesses – Sarcastic, harsh, pessimistic, critical, isolated

Scorpio-Sagittarius Cusp (November 18–24) — The Cusp of Revolution

Those born on the Scorpio-Sagittarius cusp have a source of incredible power and strength, born on the Cusp of the Revolution. This makes you capable and passionate, and you will stand up for your beliefs and fight for them.

Born on this cusp, Scorpio's planet of Pluto is the planet of death and Sagittarius' ruling planet of Jupiter, the planet of rebirth, are your influences. They inspire you to accept your personal power and right any wrongs. This is a combination of transformation and motivation that makes you so revolutionary.

You are fortunate with a Water sign, Scorpio, and the exhilaration of a Fire sign, Sagittarius, which gives you a vast array of abilities. This mix of friendliness and empathy is what makes you extremely generous. Be aware of those who look to take advantage of your charitable nature.

Those born on the Cusp of Revolution are strong and ready for action to motivate and lead. You stand by your convictions, and your sociable, magnetic attitude will have you accomplishing significant things in life.

However, a lack of freedom is something that will frustrate you and will hold you back. It would be wise to look for opportunities that will give you the independence you need.

Those born on the Scorpio-Sagittarius cusp are practical and can be somewhat rebellious. Although you like to stir the pot, others may not appreciate this, and the energy you exude can be a bit too much for some. Your energy can also make you seem standoffish or overbearing, frequently misunderstood by others. They aren't sure which person will emerge when they see you—fun and flexible or complex and fierce.

You aren't afraid to express yourself and speak your mind. You have solid standards and beliefs. You flourish with those around you who share your vivacity and strength and who can withstand you rubbing them the wrong way. You've had experience in ruffling some feathers.

You can accomplish great things with your strength and independence. These attributes can also lead to conflicts in relationships and authority figures. Direct your fierceness into determination rather than aggression, and you will go far.

Strengths – Adventurous, accomplished, energetic, passionate, benevolent

Weaknesses – Secretive, rebellious, aggressive, selfish, brusque, misunderstood

Sagittarius-Capricorn Cusp (December 20–24) — The Cusp of Prophecy

Those born on the Sagittarius-Capricorn cusp are visionaries who will achieve certain success. Born on the Cusp of Prophecy, your resilient will and forceful determination will get you where you want to go.

Your passion is fueled by Sagittarius' element of Fire, and Capricorn's element of Earth pushes you forward with intense stubbornness. The element of Fire assists your positive thinking and excitement about life, but when the fire dies out, your Earth element gives you the endurance you need to get things done and completed.

Those born on the Sagittarius-Capricorn cusp are caring, loyal, and social. There will always be people surrounding you who care and admire you and want to know what you have to say and what you think. You have a strong suit to teach others, as long as you don't become impatient or belligerent with people who learn at a slower pace.

You are a hardworking person who wants to prosper and succeed. You are motivated and want to climb to the top. However, take care because your concentrated focus can develop a division between you and those you love. You may end up lonely because your uncompromising and independent attitude is too busy changing the world.

You have all the possibilities you can imagine at your fingertips if you're born on the Cusp of Prophecy. Be appreciative of the determination and natural energy that is your gift, but use it for good.

An honest difference can be made by you as long as there's a plan to get where you're going. You'll be the leader and teacher you were meant to be if you remember to show concern for others and enjoy yourself on the way to the top.

Strengths – Responsible, friendly, loyal, successful, humorous

Weaknesses – Impatient, uncooperative, selfish, moody, closed, intense

Capricorn-Aquarius Cusp (January 17–23) — The Cusp of Mystery and Imagination

Those born on the cusp of Capricorn possess contrasting energies that make you distinctive and unique. Born on the Cusp of Mystery and Imagination, you are a hardworking optimist.

These signs of Capricorn and Aquarius are very different. However, the combination provides the ability to see the world in an unequaled way. The planet of lessons and limits, Capricorn's ruling planet Saturn, urges you to have a practical look at life and take care of your real-world obligations. Adversely, Aquarius' ruling planet of Uranus leads you to have an open mind of others around you. When blended together, these two abilities can make for a creative, striving, and potently brilliant person.

The two elements, Capricorn's Earth, determined and stable, and Aquarius' Air, desire spontaneity and variety. The challenge for you is to tend to both sides of your personality. If your energies can be channeled properly, you'll be able to succeed in any situation.

There is quite a bit of excitement internally for those born on the Cusp of Mystery and Imagination. Your mind is always racing and rolling out ideas and thoughts that are interesting. Be aware, however, that you may seem to be uninterested or detached by situations and people around you because of the continual dreams and fantasies streaming through your mind.

You love to have stimulating conversations, and people enjoy talking with you. You love to talk about problems and how there are ways to fix them. This may make you a fascinating communicator and conversationalist, but when it comes to catching up with those who care about you, it can be isolating and intimidating.

Don't forget to check in with those family and friends to see how they're doing while you share your opinions about issues regarding the world with others.

When you aren't working hard with your social networks and creative ideas that bring purpose and exhilaration to your life, remember that even the best of ideas need support from those around you who are supportive. Put extra time and effort into bonding and appreciating the people in your life.

Strengths – Creative, determined, idealistic, compassionate, entertaining

Weaknesses – Detached, selfish, standoffish, chaotic, disapproving

Aquarius-Pisces Cusp (February 15–21) — The Cusp of Sensitivity

Those born on the Aquarius-Pisces cusp are full of creativity and compassion and are blessed and cursed by feeling the weight of the world.

The Aquarius-Pisces cusp feels Aquarius' ruling planet of Uranus that brings out the progressive energy and your eccentricity, as well as Pisces' ruling planet of Neptune that advocates the acceptance of your imagination and dreams.

The Aquarius-Pisces cusp individual is friendly, peace-loving, spiritual, artistic, and extremely original. This cusp is usually labeled as eccentric or unconventional. You have a high intellect, but you can be a bit scattered and not good with follow-through and details. You are intensely intuitive and probing into philosophical ideals and matters of the spiritual nature are more significant than taking care of the details of daily life.

You are very sensitive, especially to the world around you, yet you're very strong emotionally. You're in tune with others around you, and you are in tune with their needs, hopes, fears, and feelings. The Aquarius humanitarianism, blended with the empathetic Pisces, takes understanding and compassion to a higher level.

You soak up the feelings of the people around you and have a real need to help others. Just remember to take care of your own needs and feelings as well.

Sometimes the feelings and emotions of the world can be harmful and can make you feel overwhelmed or depressed. Give yourself the same love you give to others.

Strengths – Empathetic, generous, intuitive, creative, understanding

Weaknesses – Isolated, depressed, detached, insecure

Pisces-Aries Cusp (March 17–23) — The Cusp of Rebirth

Those born on the Pisces-Aries cusp are dreamers, and go-getters all rolled into one! The last sign of the Zodiac is Pisces, and the first sign of the Zodiac is Aries, thus making this the Cusp of Rebirth. You are impulsive and imaginative, and you know what you want and want it immediately, if not sooner!

The Cusp of Rebirth is influenced by Pisces' ruling planet, the fantastical Neptune, and Aries' ruling planet, Mars. Neptune heightens your imagination, and you'll get motivated with an initiative with active Mars. You are an individual who is creative and takes the dreams you have and put them into action. Your wishes become your realities because you know how to make them come true.

The empathy and intuition of Pisces' element of Water and Aries' element of Fire are a steamy mix. Your emotions are deep, as are your beliefs, and you want to share them with the world. Not everyone thinks the way you do, so if others don't agree with you, don't take it personally.

Born on the Pisces-Aries cusp, you're strong and instinctive. This combination of energy gives you the opportunity to combine your compassion for others. You can become a successful leader because of this blend of energies. Your friends and associates will know your loyalty, and there can be some who will climb to the top with you.

You can be impatient, and your impulsiveness is joined with your intuitive knowledge. Your impulsiveness, sometimes, does not allow you to think things out, and you get into action as soon as your ideas come to you.

Your birth on the Cusp of Rebirth provides you with an ardent imagination that lets you create different and new stories, theories, and opinions. You are an ingenious pioneer who takes the best arrangement and understands the needs of others. Concentrate your energy and use the abilities you have wisely. You will be an impressive force of nature to reckon with.

Strengths – Driven, intuitive, smart, creative, quirky, fun

Weaknesses - Impulsive, selfish, uncompromising, stubborn

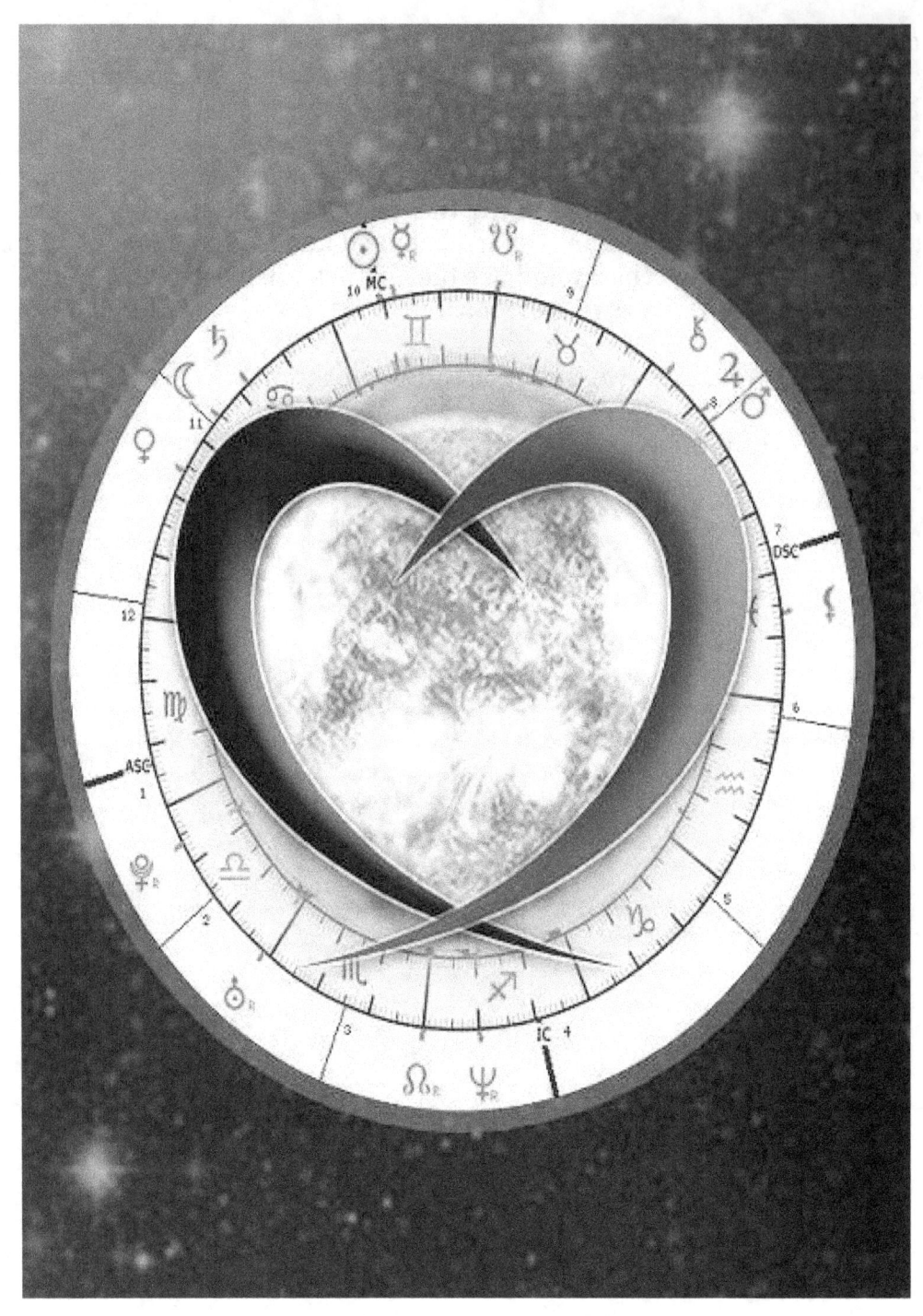

Love in the Stars

Chapter 8: Are You Compatible?

Love is a powerful emotion and one reason that makes astrology popular with people who want to better understand their love compatibility. We, as human beings, have sought love in one another for many reasons.

Many of us look for true love that will complete us and be our one and only match, while others approach love and its power differently and believe in many loves; that it is not the love of another that completes us but the love for ourselves.

These different approaches can be explained by understanding the astrological love sign and investigating what answers the stars give us at our birth.

Astrology can reveal quite a bit about who we are and how we relate to others. This is significant to know when delving into a horoscope compatibility love match.

A great tool for helping you find the right love for you is the Zodiac love compatibility tool. It can help you learn why you are attracted to one person and not another, even though they may both have all the things you look for in a romantic partner. Your love horoscope compatibility may be the answer as to why that intense desire or special spark is missing.

Astrology and its complexities help make love compatibility a science. The answer lies in the astrologers and those of us who look to the stars.

Love Secrets of Venus

The sign position of Venus discloses the "role" we take on when we want to entice love. However, it goes beyond just flirtation, and we do not "act" or facilitate a show. The traits of our Venus sign are honest traits that come from within. They are highlighted and strongly activated when we are in love.

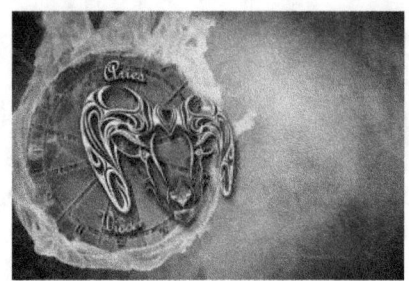

Venus in Aries

Venus in Aries people do their flirting by being direct, daring, and up-front. They express how independent and resourceful they are and try to win you over with this information. Their style of expressing love can be "me-centered," which can be maddening. However, the right person will find this charming. Aries' aura of childishness and impatience and the aura of innocent charm are things that turn some people on.

Women and men with Venus in Aries have a fun-loving, childlike manner in love. They love activity and energy and are turned on by both. The turn-offs are relationships that they consider too "mature" or stuffy, ducking the issues and being too vague. Venus in Aries people are utterly addicted to the conquest when they're in love. They need a lot of stimulation for a relationship to retain its freshness.

In order to please Venus in Aries, their need for action has to be fueled. Be open, honest and direct with them. Unless it's for fun, they're not going to play games or evasiveness. Their need for spontaneity and playfulness needs to be appreciated. Acknowledge their wish for wanting the relationship to remain fresh and young.

Pander to their many whims, and understand that they flourish on competition, even if they're competing with you.

Venus in Taurus

Love for Venus in Taurus encompasses creature comforts and the physical world. They adore their surroundings to be sensual. They express themselves as comfortable and solid. There is something about their way that promises they will be pleasing partners and lovers. In their relationships, they need a particular measure of dependability and predictability.

Women and men with Venus in Taurus have a tendency to be possessive in love and are threatened by high-energy situations in the framework of love and relationships. There are lots of expressions of love for this sensual Venus in Taurus. Their lovers may grumble about becoming a little too settled and comfortable. They do struggle with change in their relationships, but even when they seem wedged in a groove, there is always the reassurance that Venus in Taurus partners are constant.

In order to please Venus in Taurus, you need to emphasize their worth to you and your loyalty to them. They won't readily give in to you in the matters of love, so just give up and give in to them. Do comfortable things and get physical with them. Give them time to fall in love; there's no need to push them. Learn to develop patience if you're in a relationship with Venus in Taurus. Be natural and simple; promise them a cozy, comfortable time. They'll appreciate it.

Venus in Gemini

Venus in Gemini people will display how much they know to exhibit their varied interests and will try to win over the love interest with witty conversation. They are playful lovers, and some might say they like to tease. They're not easy to pin down and have a resistance to relationships that become too comfortable.

Women and men with Venus in Gemini are not in the market to become bogged or tied down in their relationships. The type of love they appreciate is lighthearted. You may get the feeling that although they will talk about the relationship, they'll avoid the deeper issues.

Their tastes change from one day to the next or, in some cases, from one hour to the next! It can be hard to know what to expect. Remember, Gemini is the Twin Sign of the Zodiac, and it doesn't necessarily mean that the twins are identical. And be aware that each "twin" may have another twin. You are forewarned!

In order to please Venus in Gemini, show interest in their knowledge and braininess, giving them their space for activities and friends outside the relationship and their need for variety and fun. Tell them how much fun they are and that you have fun with them. Don't get overly annoyed by Venus in Gemini's fickle, changeable ways. Time spent with your lover will be stimulating and exciting.

Venus in Cancer

Love for Venus in Cancer is predictable and best when it is committed. They are sensitive in love. Their egos are a bit underdeveloped when it comes to love, but they have care, comfort, and security to give.

Women and men with Venus in Cancer exhibit their love by caring for you. Their attention is more on your feelings than your words, and they watch you pretty carefully. They want a solid, safe relationship. There are times they can give you the silent treatment and be moody, using pouting routines for attention. Anything impersonal turns them off, and you leave them cold with too much explaining and rationalizing. Confrontation doesn't frighten them. Yet, they get worried about being left alone. There are times when they'll withdraw, and it can take a while and some work to pull them out.

To please Venus in Cancer, it takes a lot of sentimentality and cuddling. Acknowledge their attachments to home and family. Always make them feel cared for and secure, and they will reward you with a dependable, patient, and loving partner.

Venus in Leo

Venus in Leo people are boastful and proud to be in love. Venus in Leo loves to be courted and needs to feel exclusive. They are impressive, generous, and warm. Love is the most important in Leo's life, and they are very loyal to their partners. They blossom on romantic attention. They will tell you about anyone who makes advances on them, but you do not need to worry; they're just showing off their allure, and it's most likely harmless. However, don't do the same thing. That's when Leo the Lion will roar.

Women and men with Venus in Leo are quite big-hearted about almost everything. They do have high expectations. If the relationship has settled too much or lost the spark, they'll feel threatened. If you are indifferent or impersonal in your attitude toward them, they will feel threatened as well.

Pleasing Venus in Leo has you paying quite a bit of attention toward them. Remind yourself to let Leo know how wonderful they are. Do this daily. Appreciate and respect them. They tend to lose interest when they sense a loss of interest from their partner. Remind them that you have feelings, and your emotions count as well. When Venus in Leo feels appreciated and loved, you will be rewarded with their loyalty, plenty of physical expressions of their love, and a great sense of fun.

Venus in Virgo

Venus in Virgo people have an appeal that lies in their inclination to work on a relationship and make it work in real terms. They won't try to impress you with impressive promises or gifts. Their gifts are those of commitment and attention to you.

Women and men with Venus in Virgo slowly and quietly make their way into your heart. They are somewhat insecure and very sensitive, and this loner-like quality is part of their appeal. They need to feel confident that you like them before they make any moves, and they would prefer to play it safe in their relationships. They learn all your idiosyncrasies and are great listeners. They sometimes display their love by criticizing and nagging. Although they're calling out the flaws in your thinking, plans, or character, they're not trying to hurt you. They are actually trying to help.

To please Venus in Virgo, you need to show appreciation for all the things they do, and they do quite a bit. They do things quietly, and you may not notice and give them credit. They appreciate being given some space, so give it to them; they'll thank you for it. Be real, not affected or showy. Take care of their basic needs, and you'll find they're pretty easy to please. They're shy, so take it a step at a time in introducing them to your family or friends. They like to please and can be easily intimidated by the experiences you've had. Express how much you value and appreciate them, and you'll be rewarded with devotion.

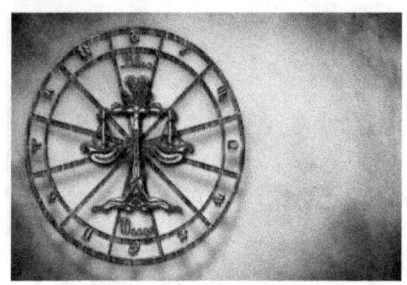

Venus in Libra

Venus in Libra people will try to make an impression by being willing to make your relationship work, their impartiality, and their kindness. Theirs is a manner of love that is polished, which can appear to be superficial or disingenuous. They treat love gently and don't like being offended. They are intimidated by a direct or abrasive exhibition of feelings and by bad manners. They look for the middle ground in their relationships. Venus in Libra's way to accommodate you by adjusting their lives may turn you on, and you can always expect to be treated fairly.

Women and men with Venus in Libra have views of their relationships that are idealized. If they feel they are being taken advantage of, they can become resentful. They make it easy for someone who is more aggressive to bully them around.

In order to please Venus in Libra, you need to treat them fairly and with kindness. Let them share everything with you. They love to converse with you about the relationship, so foreplay may be mental. They get turned on by sharing and turned off by uncouth or insensitive behavior. An imbalance in the relationship will make them unhappy, and they may have a subtle way of getting even. Don't let your relationship become imbalanced, and you will gain a reward with a lover who treats you exactly how they would like to be treated.

Venus in Scorpio

Venus in Scorpio people have been willing to commit; they are very intense, which draws others to them. Their feeling runs deep. Their promise of sexual pleasure and deep commitment will be revealed to you in their actions rather than their words. Their appeal is in their dedication and focus on you. They are fearless in being intimate, and a potential lover will feel as if they will never look elsewhere. They are extremely loyal to the person they love. They make it extremely attractive to be possessed.

Women and men with Venus in Scorpio give you their undivided and complete attention. They are focused on their partners. You may find this trait either entirely flattering or unsettling. Their need to control their partner is strong, but it won't be immediately obvious, and they may not confess to this. This may make loving them a burdensome experience because of the intensity of commitment and love. If you're looking for a lighthearted relationship, this isn't the one for you. They can be provocative and take things to extremes. They like exploring and knowing all about you but aren't as forthcoming about themselves. If they become upset with you, you won't have to guess—they'll be happy to let you know. Be aware that they're not fearful of being devious when it comes to matters of the heart and are specialists in cutting through the nonsense and see you for who and what you are. You may find their assumptions a bit mistrustful.

In order to please Venus in Scorpio, you need to exhibit your loyalty and entire commitment to them. If it's possible and you feel they are deserving, let go of some of the control in the relationship. Give them the feeling they own you; just don't allow it to go to extremes. However, Venus in Scorpio lovers will be understated in the ways they take advantage of you to keep you all to themselves. Allow them their quietness and mystery.

Venus in Sagittarius

Venus in Sagittarius people need to feel they can increase their horizons and grow through their relationship when they are in love. They want new experiences and learn new things together with you. They want you to realize their ideals, beliefs, and visions. They don't commit as easily as others in their relationships.

Women and men with Venus in Sagittarius draw others to them with their laughs and smiles, jokes, their dreams, and their friendly, playful manner. They have open minds and are proud of that fact, but they can be judgmental as well.

If their lover is dull, has inhibitions, and is over-emotional, they feel threatened. When the relationship hits rough spots, they have the urge to run the other way. They need to get out and do something new before they return, but their exit can sometimes be for good. Their attraction to people is for those who are in love with life.

In order to please Venus in Sagittarius, give them plenty of room to grow in the relationship. Learn to laugh, but don't laugh at their rants and tirades. Evade criticizing their principles, philosophizing with them, and joining them in debates. Don't force them to commit or corner them.

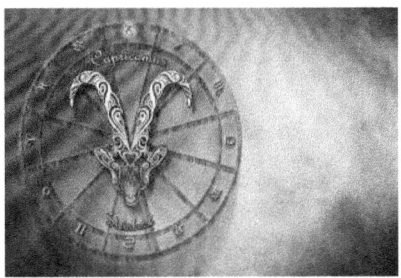

Venus in Capricorn

Venus in Capricorn people will display their responsible manner, self-control, and presence of mind, which is how they'll try to win your heart. They are savvy, controlled, and goal-oriented, and they want you to know it. They're careful in love, and some degree of expectedness is what they like.

Women and men Venus in Capricorn project an air of being capable, and their reclusiveness can be appealing. Venus in Capricorn can be a bit too deliberate and practical, and their lovers may grumble about that. They can give the impression that they're not spontaneous and lack warmth. Actually, they can be a romantic who desires a mate to share their lives with. They are attracted to goal-oriented and serious lovers.

In order to please a Venus in Capricorn, you need to show them you're realistic and sensible. They want to make an impression on you with the things they do.

They'll like to show you off to their family and friends and let you know you're a keeper.

Venus in Aquarius

Venus in Aquarius people want to make an impression on you with their futuristic thinking and open-minded spirit. They want you to realize that they're a bit provocative, rebellious, and unique. When they're acting standoffish, they're attractive. In matters of love and the heart, they want you to know they follow the beat of a different drummer.

Eccentric or unusual relationships entice women and men with Venus in Aquarius. They are not followers of the rule, yet they make a few of their own. They don't like restrictions of any kind and can appear to be aloof at times. Lovers who are the emotional type are not their cup of tea. They want to be loved for their intellect and to approve of their visions. They shun displays that are too emotional or confrontational. Venus in Aquarius will take pleasure in shocking you with their forward-looking thinking and curious ways.

When you want to please Venus in Aquarius, you need to tell them how intriguing they are. Accommodate their sporadic need to act lofty on an intellectual level. They take pride in their distinctive visions and ideas. Don't repress them or fence them in. Instead, dream along with them. They need breathing space, and they'll be very happy to give you lots of room to breathe, so you can be yourself.

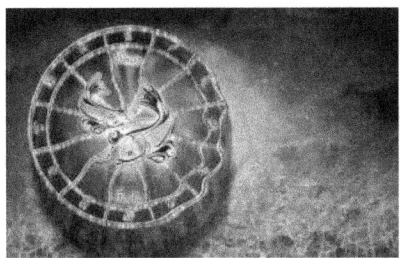

Venus in Pisces

Venus in Pisces is a sensitive and dreamy partner. The way they flirt promises a delightful time. They can be playful, irregular, and a bit moody, and their charm is elusive. They value poetry and romance and like to explore both the relationship you share and you, so don't expect planning ahead. They are sensitive, and that sensitivity is directed toward all mankind, as well as themselves.

Women and men with Venus in Pisces give love unconditionally. They are not impressed by any status you may or may not have, and they accept and love you for who you are inside. They are attracted to rebellious souls and love the "runners up." With their romantic views, they can find states of martyrdom and suffering appealing. Pisces like inequality; it turns them on! They find it difficult to commit as much as they want to.

In order to please Venus in Pisces, enjoying romantic times and tender moments with them are things they like. They may stretch the truth occasionally and do so because they don't like to hurt you. Try to recognize that about them, although it won't always be easy. They won't always be dependable. Some Venus in Pisces will have a love affair with the impression that they may be misunderstood. They are receptive and open to all options, making it difficult for them to commit to any idea, thing, or person. These partners are intriguing and will recompense you with a love that comes close to unconditional as anyone can get.

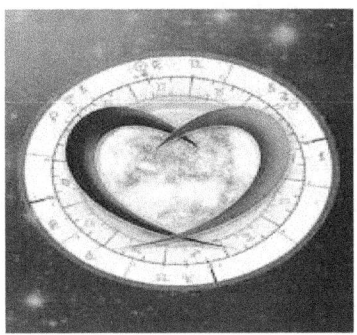

Chapter 9: How to Read Your Daily Horoscope

Are you one of those people who sit down with a cup of coffee, tea, orange juice, or a power drink, opens the newspaper or pops open the tablet or phone, and reads your horoscope to see what your future will be for the day?

Well, you're not alone because there are quite a few people who do the same thing. Approximately 70% of the population read their horoscope every day. Some may even read more than one horoscope. They may read it from more than one publication or website. (Schwimmer, Larry, 2015)

Why Do People Read Their Horoscope?

People read their horoscope for several reasons. Some people read it because they do believe that astrology is a predictor of their future. Some read it just for fun. Regardless of the reason that they read their horoscope, approximately 90% are not reading it correctly.

Most people reading their horoscope know what their Sun Sign is based on their birthdate. Every day, they go to their favorite horoscope website, newspaper, or magazine and read what's written for the Sun Sign.

If they're a Leo, they look up their Leo Sun Sign and read what the horoscope for that sign is for the day. That's it. They ponder on what they've read, and they move on to the next thing going on in their life.

This is not the way to read your horoscope. You have read only one aspect of your horoscope. You're not reading about your whole self. The Sun Sign applies to not only you but millions of other people. It's someone else's life you are reading about.

This may be a bit confusing, but the fact of the matter is, there are more signs that come into play in your astrological (natal) chart that is an integral part of who you are and lend themselves specifically to your horoscope.

Reading about your Sun Sign in the horoscope is reading the basics. You're reading about your identity but only a segment of it. The information you're receiving is valuable and covers the themes that are general and happening for all those who share your Sun Sign. Sun Sign astrology is used to develop a daily Horoscope for all the media outlets, websites, and periodicals to draw readers.

Let's face it; there are millions of people who share your Sun Sign. They can't all be having the same experience that you're having. They're reading the same horoscope that you are, but they are not the same as you and vice versa. Yes, you're all born under the same Sun Sign, but there are different aspects of your astrological makeup that precludes them from having the exact same experience that you have any day of the week, month, or year. It's not possible, and any astrologer who professionally draws astrological charts and has a full understanding of the art of astrology would never suggest otherwise. The horoscope that is available every day is limited in depth and range, making them far from accurate.

How Are Horoscopes Created?

Sun Sign horoscopes are made of four elements, as we have mentioned earlier. These are:
- The 12 Signs of the Zodiac
- The Planets
- The Houses
- The Planetary Aspects

There are 12 houses in a horoscope chart. Each House has a sign that rules that House. To determine which sign begins the First House of an astrological chart, the exact time of birth is necessary.

Sun Sin astrology analysis (these are the horoscope columns that everyone reads each morning) does not necessitate an exact time, and it's not used. The Sun Sign is put at the beginning of the chart, the First House, to be interpreted.

When reading a horoscope for your Sun Sign, (e.g., Taurus), you assume the sign ruling the First House is Taurus, and the Second House would be Gemini, and the Third House Cancer, etc.

However, if your Rising Sign is Leo, according to your exact birth time, your First House is in Leo, and reading a Taurus horoscope is not the horoscope that applies to you. The horoscope for Leo is the one that does. The events written for that day will probably fit you more rather than the general Sun Sign horoscope. (Schwimmer, Larry, 2015)

The Correct Way to Read Your Horoscope

The horoscope that you read each day is based on your Sun Sign, which is established solely on your birth date, which is pretty general. You can have a more well-rounded and accurate description of your horoscope if you know your Rising Sign.

If you don't know your Rising Sign, you can find it by using your birthday (month-day-year), your exact time of birth, and the city, state, and country of birth. The Rising Sign is established where the Ascendant (rising sign) is at the 9 o'clock position of your horoscope. It is the beginning of the entire chart.

The sign at this 9 o'clock position, which is your Rising Sign, is at the cusp of the First House. The degree and sign of your Rising Sign will determine the structure of the rest of your horoscope chart.

If you want to read your "complete" horoscope daily, you need to know your Rising Sign. For example, if you're a Taurus and your Rising Sun is in Leo, the more accurate reading and interpretation of your horoscope would be by reading the horoscope for Leo, not Taurus. You can read the Taurus Sun Sign, but remember that your Rising Sign makes the difference between you and the millions of others born under your Sun Sign.

What About Your Sun Sign?

So in reading the horoscope for your Rising Sign, does it negate your reading of your Sun Sign and its importance to your horoscope forecast? No, it doesn't! Actually, the best way to read any horoscope is to combine the two horoscope forecasts and blend them into your day-to-day reality.

Your Sun Sign will offer important information about general themes, an overview of what's happening for you. The Rising Sign horoscope is what will give you more for the timing of when things will occur with better accuracy. (Maria DeSiimone, 2019)

In order to totally understand yourself and events that may happen to you in your life, the accuracy of having a consultation and natal chart drawn by a professional astrologer is a good way to accomplish this.

Your chart can be interpreted and explained to you by a qualified astrologer. Major changes that will be happening in your life can be more accurately forecast by a natal chart reading. The astrological chart is like a map that is unique to you. Everyone should consider having their chart created at least once in their life.

Chapter 10: The Effect of Astrology on Different Religions and Cultures

Are there religions and cultures where astrology is based on? Other cultures do have their own zodiac that use the planets and signs to base their zodiac on.

The Chinese Zodiac

The Chinese zodiac is a significant element of Chinese culture. For a very long time, the signs have been used to date years in a 12-year cycle of the Chinese calendar. The significance of the zodiac to the Chinese culture is that folklore and stories have had animal signs used, which have created the different traits of their personality.

Today, millions of the people in China believe these "superstitions," these predictions that are defined within the Chinese zodiac.

Using this zodiac had led some to find their partners and friends with zodiac signs compatible with their own. It has also been used to see whom they get along with and work best with.

Generally, the Chinese zodiac provides direction on how people live and conduct their lives. In influencing the community and culture of China, the Chinese zodiac plays a significant and fascinating role.

Effects on Relationships

Relationships, from friends to mates and even business associates, are based on the Chinese zodiac. Some search for others whose zodiac signs are compatible with theirs—someone they would get along with, according to the zodiac.

In the Chinese zodiac, only some animals get along with other specific animals. As an example, someone with the sign of the dog would get along with someone with a tiger sign. They would search for a person born in the year of the tiger because it states they would get along. It is believed that people born in the year of the dog and tiger have great communication.

Realize, however, that people of the same sign will not necessarily get along, although there is a possibility. Whether a relationship would be successful or not can be determined by using the zodiac.

People who would be planning on getting into something significant, like marriage, and are serious in their belief in Chinese astrology would confer with an astrologer before taking any action. They would also do the same for people they work with or be in business with. This also includes forming friendships. There are many people who have used this approach in their lives and still use it today.

Religion

The Chinese calendar is the history of what the zodiac is based on and associated with ancient religion and Chinese astrology. The religion of Taoism is influenced by the zodiac. In the beliefs of Taoists, constellations and space are used to decide a person's "future."

Chinese astrology believes that the position of the things in space can affect a person's destiny and applies to the zodiac. The sun was used to determine how all zodiac signs were going to operate according to the dates and times.

Frequently, in many zodiacs, embedded in the center is a yin-yang symbol that represents any two contrasting principles in the universe and how it all works. The religion of Taoism is where the yin-yang originated. It is the well-known symbol of Taoism that believes that "man is a microcosm for the universe."

Yin-Yang

The yin-yang links with the zodiac because it is connected with the Zodiac's five elements to read the ten stems the zodiac uses to count days, months, and years. When it is all combined, the yin-yang affects the 12 zodiac animals and their characteristics.

Buddhism is another example of how religion links with the zodiac. One of the legends in this religion tells how all the animals were chosen for the zodiac by Buddha inviting them.

The majority of people practice Buddhism, which has the greatest religious impact on China and is significantly important to Chinese culture. The structure of the zodiac and what it has become has been influenced by religion.

Other Countries Influenced by the Chinese Zodiac

The Chinese zodiac has influenced many different cultural zodiacs worldwide. Several other countries, principally Asian, were under China and its influence at one time. The Chinese Zodiac has been impactful on zodiacs in the countries of Thailand, Japan, and Vietnam.

The varied zodiacs in these other countries are about the same as the Chinese. However, there are some differences and distinctions. The differences include the selection of animals, signs, and stories of origin.

In the Japanese zodiac, instead of a pig, the zodiac has a wild boar, a cat instead of a rabbit; instead of a sheep, it has a goat.

In the Vietnamese zodiac, instead of an ox, they have a water buffalo, and in the Thailand zodiac, there is a very large snake, a naga, in the place of the dragon.

The Chinese Zodiac has had their signs used by many cultures for various uses other than zodiacs. For example, annual postage stamps celebrating Chinese culture have used the signs. Other uses have been for decoration or tattoos.

The Chinese zodiac has, in many countries, changed the way millions of people view life in association with their beliefs of the Chinese Zodiac.

Mythology — Racing to the Finish

There are many versions of this story. Some say the Jade Emperor wanted to create the Chinese zodiac and called a race of animals on his birthday. Others claim that the Buddha did this. Regardless of the details, excluding some minor particulars, the story is basically the same.

As the myth is told, the twelve animals selected for the Chinese zodiac were chosen through a race. Time measurement for the people is the reason that the race was created. In order to win, animals had to reach the finish line on the shore after crossing a rapidly current river. There could only be twelve winners.

The animals that won the race in the order they won were the rat, ox, tiger, rabbit, dragon, horse, snake, monkey, rooster, sheep, dog, and the pig. Some of the animals had unique ways of getting across the river, but they were the animals that won the race. (Washington.edu Staff, 2007)

The lunar calendar follows the outcome of the race, the rat being first and the pig last. Once the lunar calendar gets to the pig, the sequence begins again. The lunar calendar has been an important calendar for China and the Chinese zodiac. There are many parts of the world that recognize this calendar.

Chinese Zodiac

Hinduism Astrology

A very important part of Hinduism is astrology and its part of Vedanga and part of Vedic self-understanding. The Vedic period of knowledge is total science. The Astrology system is part of the ancient Vedic period. (Goravani, 2019)

Vedic Astrology is a reference to Indian or Hindu astrology, a system originating in ancient India and recognized by sages in the Vedic scriptures. It is also known as Jyotish, the science of light. This astrology deals with pattern thought to determine our destiny and future, known as astral light patterns.

The Principle of Vedic Astrology

Astrology is the science of understanding the influence of the sun, moon, stars, and planets upon living creatures. The heavenly bodies, including the planets, have an effect throughout a human being's life, and the planetary effects are "fruit of karma."

The premise of Vedic astrology is that all things are connected. Your fortune or karma is decided by a cosmic design that is predestined. You are a soul, and that soul is manifesting in a body at a very particular place and time.

Your life is a manifestation of a greater whole into which you are born, as, at certain times, flowers bloom when all the circumstances are perfectly agreeable. According to the concept of karma, it is the case with our births on this planet.

The Jyotish is a map of the planets in the signs of the zodiac. Charts are cast based on the exact moment at an exact place on earth. The place and the moment you were born to create a chart known as your birth chart or natal chart.

Astrologers claim they can know much about you by reading the chart of the heavens for the time and place of your birth. The planets and their positions in the star-based zodiac are taken, and your predictive timeline, known as "dashas," are arranged. The Vedic chart will reveal your real life, and your dashas are probably operating properly.

The Vedic astrologer looks at the signs, planets, and house placements in your chart and can "see" your personality, life events, and possibilities, both the good and the bad events and times in your life. The moments when the events develop in life are determined by the dashas. (Goravani, 2019)

The Predictive Vedic Astrology

A predictive accuracy to Vedic astrology is given by the dashas, which is greater than what is possible with Western astrology. Unique to the Vedic system, the planetary ruling periods give the Vedic astrologers a tool for precisely forecasting the changes, trends, and events in your life with a precision that is nothing short of amazing.

Vedic astrologers can delve more deeply into what's going to happen in your life and less limited to speaking about you in general terms.

Many Vedic astrology practitioners believe that it is a great source of insightful knowledge and offers a means of predicting and understanding the events of life.

Conclusion

Thank you for reading *Astrology Activated: Cutting Edge Insight Into the Ancient Art of Astrology (Understanding Zodiac Signs and Horoscopes)* to the end.

Many people end up not reading through an entire book. The book's title would initially intrigue someone, who then buys the book to read it. But before they can get through the book, a distraction would lead them to put it down and move on to other activities.

It seems that you are interested and serious about learning the art of astrology, your personal Zodiac sign, the effects of the planets on your natal chart, and how it affects your personality and the events in your life.

Before you read this book, you may not have had an inkling on how much you would learn about your birth sign and how the planets affect each sign in your astrological chart or even how to do so.

Reading about your own sign and realizing how closely you identify with its characteristics will give you better insight into how you act and react, how you decide on things, what you should be doing, and what you need to work on yourself.

It is also interesting to learn why people act and react the way they do and how much they resemble the characteristics of their signs as well.

Hopefully, you enjoyed this book and found it informative, guiding you to the art of astrology, the Zodiac, and your horoscope.

Description

Has anyone ever asked you, "What's your sign?" Do you answer them with your Sun sign? Or do you expand their knowledge by telling them not only your Sun sign but also the signs where your Ascendant and Moon are? If you do, that's pretty impressive, but if you don't, read on.

If you want to learn about the art of astrology and what the stars say about your Sun sign and the planets that influence how you act and interact with others, then this book, *Astrology Activated: Cutting Edge Insight Into the Ancient Art of Astrology (Understanding Zodiac Signs and Horoscopes)* is a must-read for you!

Astrology was first created by astronomers in the 18th Century B.C. in Mesopotamia by the Babylonians. The first astronomers studied astronomy and complemented their studies with astrology.

Astronomers created astrological charts to predict the change in seasons and celestial events that recurred every year. The combination of the astrological charts and the movements of the planets had led them to consider that astronomy and astrology are the same science for 2,000 years.

In astrology, the planets are the most important carriers of the role and destiny of a person's horoscope. Each planet has its own identity and impact of where they are at the time of a person's birth. Your Sun sign is the most prominent because it is the planet that is closest to the sun when you are born.

So many aspects of your birth can be discovered by your natal chart. Physical appearance, constitution, and health, whether you're romantic, pragmatic, mysterious, full of energy, or slow. Also, plodding can be revealed when we learn about our fully drawn astrological chart.

Today, millions of people follow and use astrology for their own purposes, whether they want to have a natal chart drawn for themselves or a member of their family. They may also have their astrology reading drawn twice a year—on their birthday and the new year.

Horoscopes are printed in nearly every newspaper or can be found on a myriad of websites online to follow each day and read by millions. There are some who plan their business dealings or trips abroad around what their horoscope says, while others read it on a casual basis out of curiosity.

Some of the highlights of Astrology Activated are:

- How the Planets affect the astrological chart and the Zodiac signs
- A review of the 12 signs of the Zodiac and which planet rules each sign
- How a natal chart is drawn, an explanation of the Houses, Zodiac signs, and each element that affects each sign

- Your Sun sign and how it relates to your birth and the characteristics that go with it
- How to determine your Moon sign and your Rising sign
- Find out if your birthdate falls on a cusp and how you're affected by both signs
- Find out if you're reading your horoscope correctly—are you just focusing on your Sun sign?
- And more……

NUMEROLOGY 2021:

Your Destiny Decoded: Personal Numerology For Beginners

SERRA NIGHT

Introduction

Congratulations on purchasing *Numerology: Decoding Your Destiny,* and thank you for doing so.

There are plenty of books on this subject on the market, thanks again for choosing this one! Every

effort was made to ensure it is full of as much useful information as possible. Please enjoy!

Are you on a search for a new dimension? A means of evaluating personal resources. If you can count on your fingers, you can easily use Numerology to find your answers. Numerology is a mystical arithmetic system that reveals character, personality, and experience through numbers' sensitive progression.

Numerology's simple arithmetic bases its surprising revelations on more than 11,000 years of coincidence, and its effectiveness was recognized by the prehistoric, the ancient Greeks, and the Elizabethan era's societies. Modernized from the sixth century BC to today. it is a fast, simple, and positive system for self-examination and mapping opportunities.

Numerology prolongs myopic vision, magnifies vision in the dark, and simply emits light when we need clarity. Numbers are not just cumulative values to be totalized by a calculator or applied to a data set's probability. We are in the era of numbers, and the duality of its importance is increasingly in focus. We are attracted to people, places, and things that vibrate with us, and most of the time, we have one or two numbers that give us luck or appear to always appear in addresses and phone numbers, no matter how often we move. When you understand the essence of numerical meanings, you can then understand the kinds of people and experiences you continually attract when you change your residence, telephone, and automobile.

Chapter 1: What is Numerology?

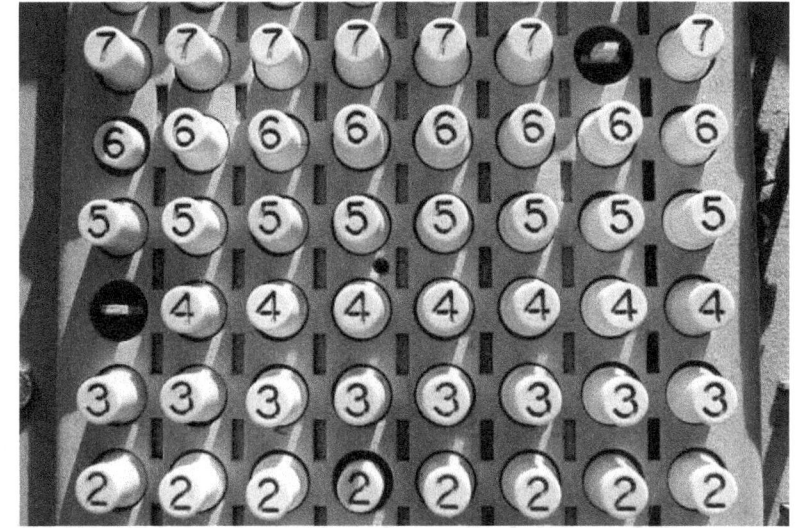

For those interested in metaphysics, Numerology can sharpen the techniques of mental expansion and prepare the mind to employ extra-sensory perceptions and mental transference easily. Numerology instigates the enlargement of the imagination. You can visualize your appearance, sensations, and actions to the maximum of your potential, based on the numbers' meanings. The ancients knew, and today's prognosticators believe that it is possible to conquer what the mind is able to visualize.

Numerology provides a complete profile of the lifestyle associated with personality when we apply the meanings of the individual numbers to the name we receive at birth and the date we are born. The numbers in our name describe the things we were destined to know. The date numbers of our birth describe the things we have to learn.

The numerical symbols of the letters in your name sketch out your instincts, self-image, and natural talents. People immediately relate to their names. Metaphysicians believe that the soul selects its name before birth to reflect the sound of its capabilities. To the listener, the name is the person's melody, to which the souls respond when pronounced. Names attract or repel according to the vibrations they emit. If you compare the numbers associated with the names of good friends and great lovers, you will find the same numbers in their respective numerological tables. Unpleasant relationships will present numbers that are not compatible. According to Pythagoras, the father of modern Numerology, this association occurs because "equal" numbers have a mutual affinity. Certain numbers that spring up continuously in someone's life, such as addresses, phone books, car plates, bank accounts, and social security numbers, come from their name or date of birth. Your birth date numbers describe the experiences of life and your goals. The date of birth's subdivisions—the day, month, and year numbers—are symbols of three main cycles of life experiences. Whereas the meaning of the total number explains the kind of people and experiences you will encounter on the way, also called destiny.

The meanings of the month and day of birth describe acts and attitudes. The month of the birth number describes the impressions and environments of youth. The day-of-birth numbers symbolize the experiences of the 27-year cycle of midlife productivity, including the period from about 28 to 36 years of age, as you mature and stabilize. The birthday number is useful at this time because it focuses on your career and explains the options. In addition, there's the challenge number. I consider this number, which is found by subtracting your birth numbers, one of the most important in a person's life because it describes how you will live with your destiny. It tells you how to use your instincts and natural talents (symbolized by your birth name number) and how to deal with the people and experiences you encounter (symbolized by your birth date number). And, finally, it is not your destiny, but your attitude that will determine success or failure, happiness or misfortune. When you use Numerology as a common-sense companion, everything becomes possible. You want to explore the greater meaning of your character, unveil disruptive habits, and gain perspective, NUMEROLOGY will answer all your questions.

Chapter 2: The Philosophy of Numbers

We believe in the inexplicable when we say, "he is number one." Why was a person "dressed in nines" when he got along? Why are we "at six and seven" when in conflict? Why is it said that cats have only seven lives? Why not 10 or 17? Is there a numerological explanation for the "seven-year crisis"? Of course, there is. When you know the meanings of numbers, these superstitions make sense.

To form a basic ground for the meanings of the numbers, let's take a look at the evolution of the numbers from 1 to 9. Pythagoras believed that the numbers from 1 to 9 led to perfection, symbolized by the number 10. Here's how it works:

- We start with 1, the idea that develops in predictable progression, step by step.
- The number 2 symbolizes the idea of opening up, being received by others, and receiving the collaboration necessary to continue to develop.
- Number 3 carries the idea to others for inspection and approval.

- The number 4 leads the idea to practical application and corrects the impracticalities.
- Number 5 adds to the promotion and exposure to public opinion. Five, the central number, opens the door to unexpected advantages and disadvantages. Here, the idea makes the transition from individual concept to community consciousness.
- The number 6 is the symbol of group participation and community responsibility. It extends the concept to serve a greater purpose.
- The number 7 is the symbol of trimming the edges, questioning and perfecting the idea until it becomes an important material result.
- Number 8 represents the life force, mental and physical organization, and practical power. It brings together body, mind, and spirit in order to produce tangible results. Ideas are formed through planning, work, and structure, applied during the influence of a number 8.
- Number 9 gives the polish, develops the skills necessary to bring the idea to the broader market, and concludes the process.

This process relates to everything we do. Ambitions develop through activities or experiences indicated by the meanings of numbers. The stages of development during the nine

months of pregnancy and the fetus' final perfection in the ninth month are a prime example of the evolution of the numbers from 1 to 9. The birth of a child starts a new life a few days after the conclusion of the ninth month. The child, a new concept, initiates the life cycle at birth and again at the beginning of the tenth month. In Numerology, the number 10 becomes a number 1 when we add 1 + 0, which results in 1. The pregnancy ends in the ninth month—9, the number of the terms. Life begins at number 1—the number of beginnings.

A Little History

Since 14,000 BC, when the Cro-Magnon man walked through the glaciers, people perceive, feel, and respond to the vibrations of numbers. Cavemen showed their interpretation of the duality of numbers with primitive designs on the floor and cave walls. The elders or leaders of cave clans gave rise to the mystery behind the counting system by refusing to expose their knowledge. The magic of numbers, as important as healing techniques, was transmitted only to the clan's most trusted and intelligent members. While crawling on the mental plane, when primeval man socialized himself, interacting with others for agriculture and barter, he probably developed counting by comparing a four-legged animal to the skins of four animals. However, the language was primitive, and man had to create sounds for numbers. He used words that allied themselves with the examples observed in his natural environment.

Primal man developed pictorial words for the numbers. The name of a six-petalled flower may have been the symbol of the word that indicated the cumulative value of six. The drawings "were worth a thousand words, which did not exist in his vocabulary."

Man's ability to communicate was limited, but he could calculate. To indicate that he had three wives, a caveman could draw a female shape next to a three-edged sheet. The observers in the clan retained the drawings and used them repeatedly. As in the children's play of the cordless phone, in which the word changes as it is passed on, it also changes the meaning intended by the caves' original artist. The use of symbols and the perception of the meanings of their combinations led to the mystical aspects of cumulative symbols (numbers that indicated more than their obvious quantity.

Modern numerology incorporates the research, imagination, and intellectual idealizations of these and other ancient societies. Around 3000 BC, the Sumerians established the sophisticated numerical system that gave us the hour of 60 minutes and the minute of 60 seconds. This knowledge was transmitted to the Babylonians, who refined it. Modern Numerology began with the Greek civilizations of the sixth century BC. All the ancients (Sumerians, Babylonians and Chaldeans, later Pythagoras and Plato, and later Renaissance believers) believed that the basic elements of tone, idea, and thought had a mathematical basis. Early Christian art was informed, through Numerology, with the Byzantine application of the six as the perfect number of creation. Six animals, six edged objects, six birds in flight were found in mosaics and drawings from that era, symbolizing perfection. From the evolution of man from the primitive caves and the glaciers until around 632 BC and the establishment of Pythagoras' numerological system, different numbers provoked new concepts. For example, the Tarot cards, precursors of the modern deck, are based on a pictorial and numerical system. The reading of the letters began when humans conceptualized intimate consciousness, built self-control, and tried to master fate. The pictorial interpretation began with a column of colored stones, which became mosaic tiles in more sophisticated cultures. The interpretation of colors, quantities, and images was inserted into a system based on coincidence—the repeated positions of the stones.

The origin of the numerical charts or when they materialized in the form of collection or deck is unknown. Egyptian, Jewish, Mexican, Indian, and Chinese archaeological excavations were found tarot decks, mosaic murals, and sculptures depicting the 22 pictorial letters that comprised the numerological system's main arcana. They were tools for evaluating character and for prediction. What they said was whispered from teacher to pupil. Leaders protected the mystical power that instilled fear in ordinary citizens.

It was the Jewish people, devoted to preserving tradition, which preserved the purity of Tarot meanings. The keys of the Old Testament's Egyptian-Hebrew scriptures in the Books of Moses (far more complex than the card reader supposes) are understood only by the Talmudic scholars. They link the numbers of the Tarot to the Kabbalah. The Kabbalah has the key to the place of the unknown vowel, necessary for interpretation. Twenty-two numbers and letters describe the primitive Hebrew alphabet. Each row of letters is also a row of numbers that sum up word, name, or expression, revealing the complexity of the Pentateuch, the Jewish writing. To this day, Jews greatly value knowledge and continue to study numbers. And thanks to the significance they give to the Kabbalistic interpretation of their scriptures, we have the documentation of a part of the evolution that led to modern Numerology. But they were not the only ones to develop a system of drawings and numbers.

The Tarot number system was also used by European gypsies, who are believed to be of Egyptian or Hindu origin and did not receive their knowledge from the Jews. Like other ancient hierarchies, Egyptian priests used their knowledge of metaphysical techniques to increase control over others. They were arrogant, kept secrets, and inspired fear in the ignorant, which depended on the birthright or the survival of the fittest. The predictions were passed on to the leaders, who used Numerology to unseat and predict the enemy's actions. There was a belief (some say also in Pythagoras) that the Egyptians and the Orientals went back to Atlantis and that from there came the knowledge of magic. Could Pythagoras have learned the "divine knowledge" and Numerology's perfections when he traveled as a young man? Fable or truth? Impossible to say because these primitive beliefs were hidden by religious secrecy and by maneuvers of power. We know that with Taro, the desire to understand self-image with drawings and numbers began. The interpretation changed over time and according to the society in which it was used. When writing began, numerical figures may have been drawn from a visual or a finger—the mental picture of the purpose of 1. For example, number 1, graphically, is standing without leaning on anything, alone. It is not difficult to understand that the numerological interpretation "independence" was applied to type 1 personality or destiny. Force the imagination and put yourself in the place of the ancients, who have been trying to make sense of things that cannot be touched, tasted, smelled, heard, seen, or spent. See how easy it would be to associate number 1 with the character of an independent person. Life opens to some number 1 destination if independence is assimilated. Challenge 1 requires a person to balance their independent actions. Could it be possible for Numerology to be born?

Systems continued to differ according to religious beliefs until Pythagoras began his Greek school of mystery. His religious belief was based on the scientific and mathematical understanding of the universal truths' relation to numbers.

Pythagoras, Father of Numerology

The charismatic Pythagoras of Samos was born in 580 BC, who dedicated his serene genius to calling forms and ideas by numbers. In an era in which humans and gods interacted, it was natural that, after his enlightening journeys around the world, Pythagoras would draw and conquer followers. He intended to elevate the man from 1 (egocentrism) to 9 (stripping). The nature of his evaluations and conclusions led Pythagoras—and later came to inspire Jesus of Nazareth—to convey to third parties the assimilated knowledge of various foreign cultures. He integrated mathematics, music, mysticism, science, astronomy, and philosophy, using them as the basis of his practical applications. Over time, he founded a religion, with school and everything, that gave support to its principles.

Revered as "the master," as "that man," Pythagoras led his followers to a "way of living." He was troubled by the thought that words did not bring a proper understanding of concepts and objects, which could be better described, he believed, by numbers.

Respectable disciples transmitted the works of Pythagoras. His convictions and theories impacted the teachings of Plato, St. Thomas Aquinas, St. Augustine, Aristotle, and Francis Bacon. There were many Greek mystery schools, but none studied, disciplined, and educated every potential disciple with the same care of Pythagoras. His school experienced human relationships and inspired, in the disciples, for many centuries, lasting loyalty.

Misunderstood Numbers

Should we refuse the extra thread in the baker's dozen to avoid a disgrace? The 13 is considered, without reason, evil. Thirteen sat down at the table of Jesus Christ for the Last Supper and followed  someone dying, sitting 13 people at a dinner table? It is rare to find the thirteenth floor in apartment buildings. But what is 13, if not 1 + 12?

For the numerologist, the 13 indicates transformation. In general, it presages the uprising and the decline that lead to the reconstruction at a higher level. When

Judas, the thirteenth at the table of Christ, began the acts that led to the crucifixion of Jesus, inaugurated the cycle of rebirth and evolution of universal Christianity. He took Christ's philosophy out of the kitchen and put it into the world. The thirteenth guest created public outcry that galvanized the followers of the entire universe. Death indeed occurred after the thirteenth sitting at the table, but the higher self of Christ lives from the religious, practical, and structured belief organized by his converts.

Thirteen is just a probation number that drives humanity to heights or depths. Numbers 13, 14, 16, and 19 are not evil but provocative. According to Christian belief, Jesus lived according to the common and basic values of honesty, truth, and love. It is said that it worked for the sake of the constructive good and did not fall prey to superficial and egocentric values (the meanings of 1 and 3, which make 13). The 13, in the numerological table, indicates proof of faith in life. It is a test of the number of its sum, 4 (13 = 1 + 3 = 4). Therefore, Numerology believes that the number 13 draws successes and failures that lead to an ordeal of economy, self-discipline, and positivity—with emphasis on work. The number 13 requires practicality, good judgment, and dedication to work for constructive values. Person number 13 always has reconstruction options.

The 13th was divine and powerful to the ancients. It is a number misunderstood nowadays, simply explainable as an exceptional number of influences, which requires the simple and objective desire to ignore superficial values and frivolity. Numerology always provides reasonable explanations for numbers that have historically been the focus of attention.

Chapter 3: How to Use This Book

- To learn the basics of Numerology, prepare to make numerological tables with the following tools in hand:
    a) Rubber pencil
    b) The draft paper for sums
    c) Add-on machine or calculator if you prefer not to add on your fingers or mentally.

- Begin by finding the uni digital number for each of the five categories of your life (challenge, automation, self-image, self-expression, and destiny).
- Write the uni digital numbers of the categories in the list of numerological categories.
- Read the meanings of the appropriate category number, listed in the chapter on the meanings of numbers in this book.
- Write down the correspondents for each of your category numbers and read how to use them in the corresponding sections.

- To analyze a personal table: compare the meanings of the challenge number with the meanings of the numbers of the most categories. Use the number-challenge meanings to identify pitfalls. Use personality categories to confirm self-knowledge. Use the destination descriptions to predict the options.
- To analyze and compare two tables: compare the category numbers to establish compatibility. Refer to the generic compatibility or incompatibility numbers listed under the corresponding.

First, learn the numerical values of the alphabet. Make at least 10 complete maps for friends and family. Record the meanings of the category numbers for each map in the book on a tape recorder. Forget the sound of your voice if it is not to your liking. Your listeners are only concerned with the words you will say about them. Be friendly. Enter the person's name. If you find something interesting or funny, demonstrate it. When you feel solidarity, demonstrate in the voice. Read the categories of personality, destination, personal year (the current year), and the personal month (the current month), in that order. Leave the meanings of the challenge to the end.

Give Numerology ribbons for engagement, divorce, or birthday gifts. You will receive positive feedback that will bring you self-confidence. The more tapes you make, the more you want to do. Repeating the reading of numeric meanings will help you remember. Decorating should not be a problem. Get into the habit of adding mentally. The key is to visualize the column of numbers before attempting to add.

Remember that 9, plus any number will keep the reduced number unchanged; therefore, it is unnecessary to add 9. Think of the name "Virlis". (V) 4 + (L) 3 + (S) 1 = 8. If we deal with I, R and I (all 9), we would have 4 + 9 + 9 + 3 + 9 + 1 = 35, and 3 + 5 = 8, however.

Using Correspondents

At the beginning of each chapter of the meanings of a number, you will find things that have vibrations corresponding to that particular number. TThere are letters, colors, foods, crystals, vegetation, instruments, and musical notes that will be familiar or receptive to people with the same numerical vibrations in their self-motivation, self-image, and self-expression or destiny. Correspondents will be valuable during years, months, and personal days that share the same numbers. When challenge numbers match correspondents, these objects detonate emotional responses.

In general, people are attracted automatically by their own numeric correspondents. It is not necessary to surround yourself with jewelry, food, colors, or music that match the numbers on your table or avoid the things that are challenges. However, your daily life can be energized with the presence of corresponding non-challenges in the immediate vicinity. Challenge objects can be corrosive.

Your correspondents appear to require actions or reactions if they match the numbers on your map. When you use, eat, listen to, or reside with objects or places with your numbers, you create your environment and focus on the people or experiences that make your life more fruitful and relaxed.

Colors, Gems, Crystals, and Vegetation

Colors, gems, crystals, and vegetation can be used to determine moods and attract help. Those that correspond to your personal numbers complement you. You should use them in the decoration of the house to give serenity, invite like spirits, or provide pleasant activities. For example, a turquoise ring on a person's token number 5 sends a subliminal invitation to people who have the number 5 in their personality numbers, destination numbers, or their mutant numbers for the year, month, and day.

Color, gem, crystal, or vegetation that match your target number should NOT be used unless you are modifying behavior and have achieved a certain balance in your personality and life. When using a correspondent challenge, expect to attract people and experiences that emotionally react to practical situations — using match-defying decorating sets challenging moods.

Color, gem, crystal, or vegetation corresponding to your self-motivation number should be used at home or when relaxing. They will attract people or experiences that leave you at ease. Your self-image correspondent should be used as an effect to improve the first impression. Your self-correspondent expression should be used to support self-expression and professional ambitions. Your destination correspondent should be used to attract new people and experiences that teach the destination number's meaning. Using colors, gems, crystals, or vegetation that match your personal year, month, or day attracts people or experiences that highlight the meaning of these numbers. Use red on day number 1 to send self-affirming vibration. It is interesting to note that, without planning, on personal day 1, many people instinctively use red color.

Food

"We are what we eat," numerologically. Foods that match challenge numbers can cause indigestion. Either you overeat them to taste them or you avoid them—there is no balance in your attitude. In certain cases, challenge food numbers can improve your health. For example, suppose people who have the number 1 challenge avoid eating the number 1 food, such as boiled beans, lobster, or chocolate. In that case, they may improve or eliminate their problems with diarrhea, cellulitis, or hernia.

If you eat foods that match personality numbers, the effect on health will be protective. The destination numbers present you with the corresponding foods—which will be offered to you, and you will want to learn about them. Mutant tastes can be identified by personal year, month, and day numbers. Foods that match your self-motivation number can be combined with other foods corresponding to the personality number. Try to use their correspondents to support the respective categories: self-help food for relaxation, self-image food to support first impressions, food self-expression in combination with the talents, food of the destination for new experiences.

Music Notes, Appeals, and Instruments

It is said that music calms the wild mood. You will find pleasure in musical correspondences related to your numbers of self-motivation, self-image, and self-expression. Correspondents of challenge numbers can be aggressive and generate emotional responses that accelerate or delay behavior modification. If you listen to the melody of your favorite romantic song, you may shed tears of depression or tears of joy. You will love or hate the challenge of musical correspondents, and you may want to use them to create a mood that puts you in touch with your feelings. Of people who cannot stand the time needed to follow their emotions and search for the reasons they are followed by melancholy, the challenge's musical correspondents may be valuable to the therapist treating them.

Chapter 4: How to Find Your Numbers: Challenge Number

This Numerology book emphasizes challenging numbers whose impact, importance, and value have not been addressed or explained in depth. Numerology gives the descriptions of challenge numbers' greater importance than the descriptions of personality numbers and fate. So, before looking up your personality and destination numbers, find your challenge numbers.

Challenge users should also read the other categories (self-motivation, self-image, etc.!) to find their challenge numbers. They may be helpful in attempting to "grate" the black and white views of the number's challenging aspect. When a challenge number is the same as that of the personality category, derived from the name or day of birth, it points to exact personality areas that need to balance the destination. When challenge numbers do not appear in other categories of personality, it is because they touch every aspect of personality.

- Challenges are best understood by the person whose name and day of birth are being mapped. They are tools for self-analysis—keys to honest self-evaluations.

- Challenges are rooted in childhood experiences. After maturity, they manifest themselves in symptoms that cloud logic and create exaggerated emotional reactions.

- Challenges are the hidden motives behind repeated mistakes and emotional extremes. They describe personality attributes that are used on the positive or negative ends. The bearer of a challenge lacks points of reference in childhood that indicate balanced behavior.

- Challenges explain the reason that you have many options. You can see a glass of water half full or half empty.

- Challenges show how to face fate. It is the attitudes of a person, not destiny, that generate success or disappointment.

"The target is the sum of reactions to our actions. So we have to change so that the target also changes" – Elisabeth Haich

Inside a Cask

There are nine types of challenges, each symbolized by one of the numbers from 1 to 9. Personal challenge numbers are found by means of a subtraction routine of the date of birth. The number-challenge meanings describe the cause, effect, and cure of inappropriate adult habits, based on the child's emotional view. These habits cause stress and affect how we face the bitter and destructive displays of black and white opinions and deeds. The gray tones of constructive commitment are illusory because they are the unknowns of childhood. The number-challenge meanings fill many gaps in our childhood and open our eyes toward happier maturity.

Find the Numbers: Challenge

Numerology has a basic rule. All double numbers are added together and reduced to a unique number, adding from left to right.

Example:

$45 = 4 + 5 = 9$

$34 = 3 + 4 = 7$

28 is captious and requires two steps.

$28 = 2 + 8 = 10$;

$1 + 0 = 1$;

Therefore, 28 becomes 1 in Numerology. The zero has a mean value, equivalent to 9, which is described in the meanings of the chapter of number 9.

Instructions for the Number Table: Challenge

Overall Step 1: Look for the day, month, and year of birth to find the challenge numbers.

Step 1. Convert the month of birth into a number by finding its place in the calendar.

January = 1, February = 2, March = 3, April = 4, May = 5, June = 6, July = 7, August = 8, September = 9, October = 1, November = 2, December = 3

Step 2. Reduce birth year to a unique number.

Example: 1937 = 2

Add 1 + 9 + 3 + 7 = 20 and reduce the unique number. 2 + 0 = THE YEAR 1937 = 2

1954 = 1

So, 1 + 9 + 5 + 4 = 19, and reduce the unique number. 1 + 9 = 10 and 1 + 0 = THE YEAR 1954 = 1

Number: Challenge System

Step 1. Fill in the unidentified numbers of the date of your birth:

A _____ B. _____ C _____

    Day   Month   Year

Note: Always subtract the smaller number from the larger number.

Step 2. B-A = _____ (Birth to 28 years of age)

Step 3. A—C = _____ (After 28 years of age)

Step 4. Subtract the remaining B-A from the rest of A-C: _____

All Life)

Step 5. B—C = _____ (All Life

Example: July 12, 1937, is the date of birth of Bill Cosby.

12 (1 + 2) is added and becomes 3 = 3

July is the 7th month of the calendar = 7

1937 = 1 + 9 + 3 + 7 = 20, and 2 + 0 = 2

Step 1. Bill Cosby's birth date with numbers: 3 (day 7 (month 2 (year

Step 2 7-3 = 4; his biggest focus is on youth and middle age.

Step 3. 3-2 = 1; your biggest focus is on middle age and beyond.

Step 4. 4-1 = 3; the focus is on lifetime.

Step 5. 7-2 = 5; the focus is on lifetime.

The challenges of Bill Cosby's birth date are 4, 1, 3, and 5.

Example: 1st June 1926, the date of birth of Marylin Monroe.

Step 1. Birthday date with numbers: 1 (day 6 (month 9 (year

(1 + 9 + 2 + 6 = 18; 1 + 8 = 9)

Step 2. 6—1 = 5 of the month and day)

Step 3. 9—1 = 8

Step 4. 8—5 = 3

Step 5. 9—6 = 3

The challenges of Marylin Monroe's birth date were 5, 8, 3, and 3.

The Number Time: Challenge Time

Note that Marylin Monroe has double challenge numbers. Marylin Monroe has the 3, socially insecure and jealous of her own image. When a challenge number appears more than once, the challenge is hard to beat. The dual challenge numbers warn that influences or environments of childhood will not change with maturity. These challenges are constantly being reinforced. It is more desirable that the challenge holder digest them gradually over a long period of time. Situations will arise to focus on their meanings.

Overall, Step 2. FIRST CHALLENGE: The subtraction of the month and day gives the number that describes the challenge felt most strongly until around the twenty-eighth birthday.

Overall, Step 3. SECOND CHALLENGE: The subtraction of the day and year gives the number that describes the challenge felt most strongly in the middle, which can last and arrive until the last years.

Overall Steps 4 and 5. THREE AND FOURTH CHALLENGES: Subtractions from the remains of the day and year require lifelong attention.

Categories of Personality

Personality is divided into three categories—self-motivation, self-image, and self-expression. You'll find the category numbers of your personality, using the full birth name.

Basic Rules for Name Interpretation

To construct a map, use only the exact letters of the names printed on the birth certificate or equivalent. Nominations, baptismal names, early name changes, wedding names, and professional names should not be used in the construction of the numerological map.

Junior, Son, Grandson, etc., are not included in the name map. It is accepted that the child will have the characteristics of the name, which were the same for the first owner of the name. Uniqueness is explained through the opportunities offered by different names at birth.

Being a newborn, a boy, a girl, a teenager, a man or a woman, an initial (A., B., C., etc.) or a name that was never used but was registered in the birth certificate or album (the family Bible, etc.) of any culture, will be the name to be used in the preparation of the numerological map. It is understood that the first record has been chosen by the new soul who came to earth to fulfill its purposes.

Note: There are all sorts of logical reasons to call this numerological rule impossible, ridiculous, and crazy, and many customers have already told me, "But I never used this name ... it was a mistake." However, the para-scientists, the metaphysicians, and the numerologists believe that there is a purpose and a plan for all. There are no mistakes.

Categories of Personality: Purpose and Instructions

Automation

Your self-motivation number is derived from the numerical values of the vowels of your full name of birth. Use the name that appears on the birth certificate or another first record according to the custom of different countries and cultures. The numerical equivalents of the full-name vowels, summed up and reduced to a single number, reveal what we want, what we feel inclined to, and what we want to have to feel content. Instinctively, we dedicate our body and soul to the values described by the number of our self-motivation. It describes what we want to be and what we want from our lives.

To add depth and scope to the understanding of the self-motivation number, you should also read the numerical meaning of each individual name of the full birth name. The reduced single number of vowels of the first name indicates the practical instincts. The reduced number of vowels in the last surname reveals the bearer's spiritual instincts and the paternal side of the family. Self-motivation, on the metaphysical plane, is called the "impetus of the soul."

Self-Image

Your self-image number is derived from the numerical values of the consonants of your birth name. The unique number calculated for your full name is the most important. However, the numbers of the individual names of a birth name add to the understanding of what we want to show the world.

The self-image number reveals the impression that observers have of us when we step out of an elevator, thinking no one notices us, or when we enter a room without being announced—it is the first impression we make. And the visualization of the success that we cherished when we were young when we dreamed and planned the way we walk, talk, dress, and progress as adults. When we live according to the meanings of our self-image number, we disregard the demands of others and emit, in their place, numerical vibrations that attract our dreams. Our self-image is born in the imagination. And the key to understanding how we see ourselves at our best.

Self-Expression

Your self-expression number is derived from the sum of all numeric values of the letters of the full name. The numbers of each name are totalized separately and reduced to a number. These numbers are then summed and reduced to a number. To find the overall picture, read the meaning of the unique number of all letters' values.

Individual names in the full name of birth, when reduced to the meaning of their unique number, describe talents, potentials, and methods of self-expression. The meanings of the reduced unique numbers of first names, first names, and surnames of the full birth name should be read to obtain additional information.

The number of self-expression indicates your professional talents and sums up their capabilities. Its ingredients suggest professional choices that use material capabilities. Whether as a homemaker, hobbyist, or a dedicated professional, you'll be more comfortable concentrating on the meanings of self-expression numbers to attract recognition.

The Numbers Have a Positive Side and a Negative Side

The numerological map must be completed before reading the numbers' individual meanings because all the complex parts of our nature must be viewed as a whole. In order to fully understand a numerological profile of the personality and its destiny, we must recognize that every numerical description has a negative side and a positive side. Most people are not always positive or negative; they might not even be balanced many times.

The complexities in our nature become clear when the meanings of our numbers are read one after the other. People are not simple. We often confuse our friends and ourselves by revealing conflicting desires. A complete personality map sheds light on these dichotomies.

After reading all the personal numerical values, new options for us will appear. The possibilities, hitherto unplanned, indicated by a number of the personality category, might send flames on the Scarlet O'Haras who are among us and who "leave for tomorrow what they can do today." The definition of periods of life can detonate a sense of immediacy. Scrutinizing opportunities for life can ease the worries of those who believe that life is surpassing them.

We pack, very often, in the events of the moment. Our past efforts and our aspirations for the future may lock in when we think we are facing an emergency. It is human to use the numerical meanings of Numerology in order to find solutions to immediate problems, but it is better to return to the long-term possibilities indicated by the description of our destination number as soon as the emergency is over.

Numerology helps us understand when and how time can heal our emotional wounds or solve problems. If we wait to read the numeric meanings of the entire list of personality categories, we may discover new predicates. It may be that, for the future, there is a very well-defined chronology of events. There may be a more promising solution that reduces anxiety and gives less importance to what may appear to be a need for immediate action.

To benefit from the side view offered by numerology, it is best to map first and read later.

Destination Number: Purpose and Instructions

The destination number describes what they expect us to learn. Metaphysically speaking, the number of destiny describes our purpose on the plane of life. The types of person and experience indicated by this number will not be surprising unless the traits of self-motivation, self-image, and self-expression of the personality, or the date of birth, are the same.

If the self-expression number is the same as the destination number early in life, you will have a profession, and the experiences you encounter will accelerate your progress. If your self-motivation number is the same as the destination number, you will quickly get to know the people and experiences that will make you feel better. If your self-image number is the same as your destination number, you will have opportunities to experience the fantasies of the life you led as a child. Few people have the same numbers in the categories of personality and destiny. Most people live the "seek-and-find" method and learn from experience. By understanding the numerological meaning of the destination number, you are able to identify who you will become, what you are expected to do when the time comes, why you are here, after all, where you should seek help, and when things happen at the right time.

Instructions for Finding the Number of the Destination

Step 1: Add the numbers of the day, month, and year of birth. Or reduce the day, month, and year numbers to unique numbers and add them.

Step 2: Reduce the sum to a number between 1 and 9. The unique reduced number of the sum of the numbers of the day, month, and year of birth is the destination number.

Bill Cosby's example: July 12, 1937

12 = 1 + 2 = 3

July = 7

1937 = 1 + 9 + 3 + 7 = 20; and 2 + 0 = 2

3 + 7 + 2 = 12; and 1 + 2 = 3

OR

12 + 7 + 1937 = 1956; and 1 + 9 + 5 + 6 = 21; and 2 + 1 = 3

The destination number of Bill Cosby is 3.

The Number of the Personal Year: Purpose and Instructions

Life is divided into cycles of nine years of experience. We begin new concepts in the personal year of the cycle and conclude the goal of the first cycle eight years later in a personal year number 9. The seven years between years 1 and 9 give our initial concept. In the personal year number 9, we leave the past and prepare ourselves for a new course in the following year—personal year number 1 begins another cycle of experiences. We live in cycles of seven years, but few remember factoring the first year when ideas take shape or the last year when we abandon the idea.

During personal year number 9, we reflected on the past eight years and found that personal year number 1 goals were met. New concepts are born based on achievements or conclusions. The seed of change is planted. You cannot start and finish important projects in the same year; so when the year 9 is over, new things are instigated in a year 1. They are cultivated in a 2, they come to light in a 3, they descend to earth in a 4, they make transitions in a 5, they add responsibilities in a 6, they specialize in a 7, make material advances in an 8, and achieve recognition in a 9.

Each year of the nine-year cycle has a purpose.

Personal Year Number 1

Offers opportunities for change in the direction of progress. It's a start-up year, during which we can expect to start projects.

Personal Year Number 2

Offers opportunities to know the details of projects initiated in cycle number 1. And a year of details, receptive, during which we build the future results.

Personal Year Number 3

Offers opportunities to bring to light the goals of cycle number 1. And a year of start-up, during which we can expect to see the results of social contacts.

Personal Year Number 4

Offers opportunities to correct bad practices and build security for the future. It is a year of work, receptive, during which we build for the future.

Personal Year Number 5

Offers opportunities to try new ideas, to use various means of self-promotion, and to experience physical pleasures. And a year of start-up, transformer, during which we can expect to see results. The first four cycles of the personal year are rooted in independent acts. The fifth-year is a central cycle that opens the door to unknowns and the transition of the way of life.

Personal Year Number 6

Offers opportunities to conduct long-term intimate business and commitments, to take on obligations, and to be useful. It is a receptive year during which we build for the future.

Personal Year Number 7

Offers opportunities to be introspective and to re-evaluate intimate, business, and spiritual goals. And a solitary year, to observe, be receptive, and expect little if any, commercial result.

Personal Year Number 8

Offers opportunities to take control of material and commercial matters. And a year of problem-solving, to be very aggressive, courageous and expect high-level tangible results.

Personal Year Number 9

Offers opportunities to be philosophical, worshipful, and charitable. It is a year to be receptive to the needs of many people, to set an example, and expect the results of the original concepts shaped in the personal year number 1. And a year to clean the rotten. Nothing new begins.

Instructions to Find Your Personal Year

Method 1: Using Personal Year Quadriculates

Step 1: Look for the grid for the current calendar year.

Step 2: Look for the date of your birth (day and month) on the grid and find the number of your personal year.

Method 2: Using System Year

Step 1: First, you should look for a unique number for any calendar year. Add the calendar year numbers and reduce them to a number between 1 and 9.

EXAMPLE OF CALENDAR YEAR:

1991 = 1 + 9 + 9 + 1 = 20

2 + 0 = 2

1991 = Year of the Calendar Number 2

Step 2: Add the unique calendar year number to the numbers of your month and day of birth.

Step 3: Totals equal to or greater than 10 should be reduced to a one-digit number by adding their two digits.

Example: BILL COSBY PERSONAL YEAR FOR 1991

Date of birth: July 12

Step 1: 1991 = 1 + 9 + 9 + 1-20 -2 + 0 = 2

Step 2: Add 3 (12 = 1 + 2 = 3)

+ 7 (July, the seventh calendar month)

+ 2 (calendar year number)

TOTAL = 12 = 3

Bill Cosby was in a personal year number 3 in 1991.

Numerical Comparisons

There are several ways to use the numeric comparison on your own map or between two maps. For example, if you want to know if your talents are on a destination track that will offer immediate recognition, compare your self-expression number with your destination number. If you want to know if it's compatible with a colleague or work superior, compare your self-expression number with his. If you want to know if your first impression is compatible with the people and experiences you will encounter in life, read the meaning of your self-image number and compare it to the focus of your destination number. Common sense always helps to make comparisons and determine compatibility.

The following is a quick numerical comparison table to identify the generally compatible numbers and those that are not. But, remember, Numerology always provides choice: incompatible numbers do not have to cause frictional relationships; it is enough that partners or partners understand each other and want to make a reciprocal commitment. They are levels of incompatibility that can be relieved with the commitment of both to work together. But the first step always depends on the person who has the smallest number. He or she will have to be willing to learn from the person who has the highest number. And whoever has the highest number should make a commitment to give the smallest person enough time to learn. Communication is the key. Same numeric meanings in your table and someone else's chart can set the path to the best relationship.

However, if you are thinking of starting a long-term commitment to a person whose self-motivation and destination numbers are incompatible with yours, it may be better to agree than to disagree before problems arise.

Here are some practical rules for comparing numbers:

- When plotting comparisons between maps or on your own map, always use the final reduced number of categories for the challenge, self-motivation, self-image, self-expression, destination, year, month, and day.

- On your own map, compare your desires (self-motivation) to your talents (self-expression) to determine if you have the talent to get what you want.

- On your own map, compare your self-expression (talents) number to that of your destination to see if you will find people and experiences that will make it easier for you to contact business or profession. If these numbers are incompatible, you should focus on the meaning of your destination number to know what kinds of environments will open doors for you.

- On your own map, compare your challenge numbers to your numbers of self-motivation, self-image, and self-expression. If they are the same, you can mark the extreme part of your personality that reaches extremes and needs modification. If one of your challenge numbers equals your destination number or personal year, month, or day numbers, you will find it difficult to react to the people and experiences you encounter without putting emotion into practical situations. You can soften your life by understanding that your intense emotional reactions are detonated by the people your destination presents (you will not want to choose the wrong person to date, get married, or work). You can smoothen your life by focusing on locking relationships with people and experiences that will help you throughout the time or period in question.

- On your own map, if the single reduced number of your self-motivation is greater than your destination, this means that you want more comforts than life offers. If your self-image number is larger than your target number, you seem more accomplished than most people you meet. If your self-expression number is greater than your destination number, you have more talent than you need to fulfill your destiny. If your name numbers are less than your destination number, you need to strive to learn what life has to offer. Always remember that the numbers of self-motivation, self-image, and self-expression, referring to the name, relate to the character, and the challenge numbers, of the destination, of the year, month, and day, of birth, relate to the types of person and experience you can expect to encounter.

- When making comparisons between maps or on your own map, compare personal year numbers to month and day numbers to find out when months and days will support the purpose of the year and are not frustrating. When short periods do not lead to quick realizations, it is best to be prepared for delays and understand that the person worried about you are also experiencing difficulties.

- To determine when to enter into a partnership, a marriage, or a business, compare your personal year numbers. The number 9 is a year of terms and never starts anything that lasts. Number 6 is ideal. Whenever possible, aim to start a long-term commitment in year 6. If this seems impossible, choose to get married in a month or day number 6. In business, numbers 4 and 8 are fortunate as well. But do not start in a year, month, or day number 9. Also, be sure to read the meaning of the two partners' personal year to understand what the opportunities are.

- Always compare your personal day numbers with those of your close friends and co-workers. If you know when to be a good listener and when to give an opinion, you will effortlessly accomplish the goals of your personal day.

- The reduced single birth date can be compared between two maps to determine compatibility from approximately 28 to 55 years of age.
- Month-of-birth numbers can be compared between two maps to determine if early environments will offer clogs or unknowns, comfortable or uncomfortable reference points.

The tables of quick numerical comparisons are comfortable, but if you have the time, it is best to read the full numeric meanings and gain deeper intimate insights. When in doubt, or when you need to make a quick decision, use common sense. Numerology is a tool and a companion of struggle. Your yearly, monthly, or daily forecasts can teach you how to save time until you're sure you're doing the 'right' thing.

Chapter 5: Number 1 – Independence

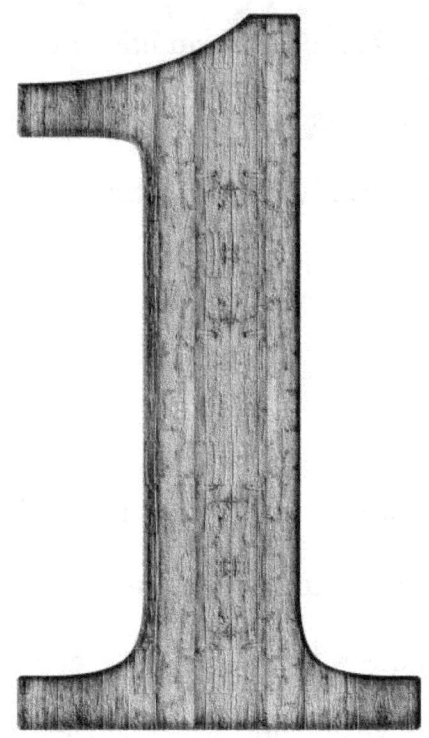

Attributes

Positive – Individuality, Leadership, Creativity, Positivity, Active Power, Ambition, Persistence, Self-confidence, audacity

Negative – Self-centeredness, authoritarianism, Imitation, Repression, Dependency, sloth, passivity, fear, weakness

Correspondents

LETTERS: A, J, and S

MENTAL AND PERSONAL ATTAINMENT NUMBERS:

10, 19, 28, 37, 46, 55, 64, 73, 82, 91, 100

COLOR: red

GEM: Ruby

CRYSTALS: Granada & Pyrite

VEGETATION: azalea, Iris, lilac

FOOD: Salad, Baked beans, Halibut, Lobster, Chocolate

MUSICAL INSTRUMENT AND/OR CALL: Piano, Opera

MUSICAL NOTE: Central

PLANET: The Sun

MONTHS: January and October

DAYS OF BIRTH: 1, 10, 19, 28

DAY OF WEEK: Sunday

GENERAL COMPATIBILITY NUMBER (S: 3, 5, 9, 11, 22, 33

INCOMPATIBILITY NUMBERS: 6, 24

Note: If the individual has no 1 challenge number, these descriptions change from positive to negative until you balance the challenge. Make sure you read the meaning of the challenge.

Challenges of the Number 1

It is a challenge to the individual's self-respect. It is rooted in excessive control or very sensitive discipline by authority figures in childhood. In particular, the father was very aggressive or was not present during the formation of the child. Perhaps, the mother was very authoritarian, playing the role of the "man" and confusing the child. Therefore, the child becomes an adult without understanding how to be comfortable alone or not understanding how to communicate to get what you want or need.

As the child grows, if independent ideas and decisions come up against criticism or overprotective worship, it will become frustrated and do things that are inappropriate for attention. You will try to please or annoy the incomprehensible parent or controlling authority. You will get into the habit of going from one end to the other. By not being able to autonomy, by wanting love, but not knowing how to satisfy personal expectations or desires, the child will be easily controllable, or angry, will try to control himself.

In youth, if the authority figure has shown excessive concern or was too inaccessible or unavailable by divorce or death, the child perceived acceptance or rejection as "he loves me, he does not love me." Infant emotional judgments, based on black and white perceptions, persist until maturity when challenges take effect. When experiencing creative ideas, when young, or emitting professional concepts as an adult, the bearer of the challenge expects to be received with disapproval or flattering exultation for utility and individualism. Challenge number 1 can swing from one to the other of the following extremes until each one of them is recognized, initiating new habits that stabilize the ego.

- Very impatient or very passive.
- Very independent or very dedicated.
- Very accomplished or very unpretentious.
- Very creative or very copier.
- Very ambitious or very lethargic.
- Very egocentric or very indulgent.

- Very aggressive or very indecisive.
- Very affirmative or very submissive.
- Very controlling or very controllable.
- Very obedient or very provocative.
- Very selfish or very generous.
- Very domineering or very obsequious.
- Very changeable or very lazy.

Physical Challenges of the Number 1

Challenges can affect physical as well as mental health. The chemistry of the body changes when individuals are stressed, and when we do not know what is good for us, our minds detonate anxious, angry, or frustrated habits. When we mistreat ourselves, we become sick. Every attitude sends a message to the brain, and the brain tells the body to scream for help.

To draw attention to their discomfort, people often become ill or form negative habits. Numerologists believe that illness and well-being depend on attitude, and challenges indicate attitudes resulting from feelings of need. When we do not feel needy, we feel good, balanced, and do not beg for the attention of others. Essentially, if personality challenges are balanced, the body's chemistry will remain balanced, too, and therefore, the risk of physical or mental illness will below.

Challenge numbers indicate how people punish themselves unconsciously for not being consciously good about themselves. The list of illnesses and negative habits to follow is related to the challenge of number 1.

- Anorexia Nervosa
- Urinating in Bed
- Bladder
- Bone problems
- Cellulite
- Circulatory Problem
- Cough
- Deafness
- Diarrhea
- Fever
- Foot Problems
- Glaucoma
- Headache
- Hernia
- Impotence
- Knee issues
- Lung Problems
- Menopause
- Rheumatism
- Hands Trembling
- Stress

Balancing the Challenges of the Number 1

The first step in balancing the challenge is to feel free to say, " I need to ... ". When you feel intimidated by authoritarian, dogmatic, or fast people, speak up. You have the right to make your own decisions because your desires are worth as much as those of others. Remember to focus on your ambitions. It is possible that you lose supporters if your ideas are unconventional but take responsibility for yourself and move on. It may take unpleasant gestures or act when others choose to wait. You have to have the courage to try out your original ideas.

If you do not try, you will never go wrong. If you do a lot of things, the odds are you will not always hit the first time. But you will learn to decide, and this is what you need. You will feel good when you realize that you have control of your life. Forget the expectations of others, dare to be yourself, and recognize that, as pioneering, ingenious, and independent individuals, "some of us have won, and some of us have lost."

Automotive

Youth:

As a child, the child feels a strong urge to stay together in their concrete world and a difficult period in their lives, of those who wish to explore. Maybe children do not usually make their own decisions, but the number one motivation often frustrates them when they cannot follow their instincts.

The solitary 1, determined, may find it difficult to adjust to the regimes adopted by troubled parents and become disobedient. Excessive restrictions may leave the child defeated, insecure, and powerless. Still, too much dependence on the child may generate fits of anger or inertia, if not tempered by the balance that stimulates individuality. Finally, for the parents, other authorities, and the child, the period before emotional and financial independence is particularly difficult.

Maturity:

Adult 1 wants to control his activities and rarely hears the advice of others. The 1 wants—although they do not need it—partners who support it. And as an accommodating loner, he plans accomplishments that, hopefully, attract praise and adeptness. As a leader and manager, the number 1 prefers to leave the details to the subordinates or another significant person. When personally or professionally involved with colleagues, he prides himself on his executive ability and easily embarrasses himself with subordinates' incompetence. When caught in personal error, the number 1 feels humiliated and takes immediate steps to keep up appearances.

For these self-sufficient and cerebral individuals, love and marriage may not be primal motivations. Numbers 1 oscillate between introversion and companionship depending on their immediate goal. They may feel bold after realizing their ambitions and deciding that it is time to start a family. When they feel the need for self-glorification, they can decide to be the center of someone's world without giving up their independence.

Balanced numbers 1 do not allow others to have them. They need to relate to supportive and diplomatic admirers, who recognize (and applaud) their originality and achievements. The wedding of two motivations number 1 will base your attraction on activity and experimentation. There is little time for individual recognition. Since the number of self-motivation describes what we need to be comfortable, the partnership of two motivations number 1 will result in two convinced aspirants seeking adjustment on the other.

Self-Image

Youth:

Lying in bed, listening to music, and wondering, "How will I be when I grow up? How will I walk, dress, and talk?" the number 1 preadolescents see themselves as future exclusive individuals. They dream of pioneering explorations of the Alps and find themselves flattered by being the first to reach the summit. Children with self-image number 1 imagine themselves as bosses, organizers, and inventors. They can be creative in supplying the dishwasher or by redesigning the vacuum cleaner. They are always in a hurry—planning ambitious adventures, eager to reach the independence that maturity offers.

They always seem to stand to take the lead. They are more attracted by the instigations than by the detailed work or the good finishes. They strive automatically to get others to work for them. Therefore, number 1, teenagers should be encouraged to see themselves performing tasks from start to finish and not just whipping others or promoting the end result.

Maturity:

Upon exiting an elevator or entering a room-before the personality or intellect takes action, the adult number 1 emits vibrations of being different and being in movement. Their attitude indicates strength, and they seem to transpire vitality.

Number 1 adults perceive themselves as commanding people. By living according to their self-image, the first impression they make implies strength, mastery, and self-affirmation. The number of self-expression can govern the first impression if career requirements, included in the meaning of the number, indicate uniforms, stylized functional dress codes, or fashion.

Self-Expression

Youth:

Adults find it obvious when children have 1 as a self-expression number. The young number 1 believes in leadership and that some of their trusted followers will support their game. When they grow up, others will stick to them when the authorities choose them to hold leadership positions. Sometimes they may seem like tyrants, alienated, and discreet adults at the same time. The 1 is affirmative, instigating, and egoistic energy. It's hard for them to stand still for a long time without boredom and innovative suggestions.

The number 1 talents take these kids to the director's chair. They will be more capable adults if they can develop in their own cadence and in their own way. Their creative ideas will immediately move the authorities. If praised, the inquisitive mind number 1 will elaborate on new projects.

Maturity:

Suggested Occupations: Inventor, designer, salesman, pilot, explorer, architect, buyer, seller, actor/actress, director, promoter, writer, publisher, conductor or musician, contractor, illustrator, cartoonist, politician, or any career that requires independent action, as well as a career that requires independent action, leadership and originality.

Destiny

This destiny indicates a life of self-development. To make the most of Numerology's farsightedness, Number 1 should never expect to depend on others. The individual may prefer to follow leaders in their youth. If one does, one is usually placed in subordinate positions until one becomes indispensable.

Personal Year

Year 1 is the first year of the nine-year cycle of experience and results in the challenge of qualification and performance based on your goals. It's time to shock conceptualized ideas three years earlier. For most, the people and experiences found this year promote rebirth. For the others, the year focuses on promoting new schemes and adds larger dimensions to current interests. Personal year number 1 allows the individual to tie, between January and August, the ends that remained loose in the previous year. The intensification of activity and the clarity of purpose increases in September—month number 1 in year number 1.

Change and independent thinking are key issues in this powerful year. This is no time to settle in or hesitate. The year begins slowly and provides the events with surprising twists and turns that, in April, change the ideas. July offers the individual a chance to take control—to plan, build, and act. This act then establishes the stage of abandoning previous commitments in August.

September's activities intensify new perspectives and the need for change. Between September 21 and 30, the individual must check the impracticalities and open the way to the new long-term ambitions.

Personal Month

The personal month number 1 of any personal year is operative, and the 1 must take the initiative. And the month in which the things that were about to be completed three months ago are carried out, but not materialized. Situations will arise this month that will put the individual in the driver's seat. New people, situations, and ideas abound. The 1 must be aggressive and use the period to make changes. Decisions should be based on independent and intellectual assessments since aid and encouragement should not be forthcoming. On the whole, the focus should be on beginnings.

Personal Day

Wake up with a determined attitude. Whether you are heading for a new job, a prospect, or any situation you want to promote, a smart new approach will open doors that have been closed. Extra-sensory perception is working, use intuition, stick to convictions, and do not lose control. The outlook will be new; therefore, grasp the opportunities that the day offers to be original.

You will be surprised to note that ambition, self-confidence, and creative thinking are all in the air, and you will feel satisfied today. Activate today's energetic and independent state of mind by wearing a tie or a red outfit. Above all, do not be lazy. Carefully plan all personal appointments and make sure you have a set goal. Stay tuned and use the practical evaluations to see your ideas complete. Because this working day has a purpose, it must be used decisively to begin something new.

Chapter 6: Number 2 – Cooperation

Attributes

Positive – Contributor, attentive, Diplomatic, Emotional, Compassionate, Responsive, Adaptable

Negative – Insensitive, pusillanimous, Impolite, Careless, critic, Shy, Fearful, disinterested, indifferent, Sly

Correspondents

LETTERS: B K, T

DISPOSAL: Concerned emotionally and personally

MENTAL AND PERSONAL ATTAINMENT NUMBERS:

11, 20, 29, 38, 47, 56, 65, 74, 83, 92, 101

COLOR: Orange

GEM: Adultery

CRYSTAL: Rutile

VEGETATION: Eggs, Poultry, Sheep, Nuts

INSTRUMENTS/MUSICAL APPEAL: Zeal, Organ, Aria

MUSICAL NOTE: D (When tuned, C sharp

PLANET: Moon

MONTHS: February and November (Shared with the number 11

DAYS OF BIRTH: 2, 11, 20, 29 (11 and 29 are shared with the number 11

DAY OF THE WEEK: Monday

NUMBERS GENERAL COMPATIBILITY: 2, 4, 6, 7 (8 in the business plan

NUMBERS INCOMPATIBILITY: 5 (9, in commercial terms

Note: If the individual has the number challenge 2, these descriptions will go from positive to negative until the challenge is balanced. Please be sure to read the meaning of the challenge.

Challenges of the Number 2

It is a challenge to the individual's sensitivity, perceptions, and susceptibility. It has a root in precocious attention too much or scarce with the feelings and the emotional reactions of the bearer of the challenge. The woman, generally the mother, either is very supportive and is too involved or is absent because of illness, divorce, or death. The father may have been very kind and receptive, and have played the role of the 'woman,' which may have unbalanced the child. Therefore, the baby becomes an adult without understanding whether to expect too much, too little or how much, indulging in intimate relationships.

It is difficult for children with challenging 2 to reach maturity by relying on themselves. They do not recognize their exclusivity, nor do they imagine living or working alone. These children are often indecisive because of their talent for seeing all the details on both sides of the same coin.

The No. 2 challenge users expect from themselves and their loved ones too much self-sacrifice. If the father or mother was a martyr, there is already a marked example that these children must overcome. As adults, the 2 always put themselves at the disposal of others. They back off and refuse to give up anything again. It is difficult for those in Challenge 2 to realize that they are not the only ones to have been bothered by sadness, loneliness, or malaise.

How do challenge 2 people abandon their defenses, break habits, and throw away misrepresented childhood impressions? First, they must remember that the universe does not revolve around themselves, their sensitivities, or their emotional relationships. Their defensiveness, surprisingly, establishes habits that put their personal feelings above the rights of others. Challenge number 2 can swing from one to the other of the following extremes until it is recognized and new habits that stabilize the sensitivity of the challenge bearer begin.

- Too sweet or too bitter.
- Very personal or very impersonal.
- Very open or very closed.

- Very grumpy or very grateful.
- Very humble (apologizes) or without remorse.
- Very helpless or very helpful.
- Very attentive or very rude.
- Very honest or with two faces.
- Very clement or very evil.
- Very hurt or too hard.
- Very dependent or very lonely.
- Very soft or very rough.
- Very friendly or very cold.
- Very unhappy or very loving.

Physical Challenges of the Number 2

A person's attitude sends a message to the brain that tells the body to scream for help. In order to attract attention to their malaise, people usually get sick or form negative habits. Numerologists believe that illness and well-being depend on attitude, and challenges indicate attitudes that result from feelings of need. When we do not feel needy, we feel good, balanced, and do not beg the attention of others. Essentially, if the personality challenges are balanced, the body's chemistry will also be balanced, and therefore, the likelihood of mental or physical illness will be small.

Challenge numbers indicate the ways in which people punish themselves for not being consciously generous to themselves.

The list of diseases and negative habits below relates to the challenge of number 2.

- Athlete's Foot
- Multiple Sclerosis
- Birth Defects
- Early Burns Leg Syndrome
- Restless
- Circulatory Problems
- Sciatica
- Diabetes
- Problems of Throat
- Fevers
- Tonsillitis
- Foot Problems
- Tuberculosis
- Hair Loss
- Urinary Tract Infections
- Hepatic Stains
- Vaginitis
- Menopause Problems

Balancing the Challenges of the Number 2

The first step in balancing the challenge is to feel free to say, "I need kindness." Ignore the insults and pessimism of the past. Forgive and forget. Always expect the best. Use a gentle way of asserting yourself without going to the extreme of prefacing every request with numerous and exaggerated greetings. If you are aware of yourself, remember that others want to know what you think of them. We all seek approval; therefore, stop criticizing. The reflector is not always aimed at you.

When you're out of time for yourself because you're a slave to others, remember that supporting, sharing, and collaborating does not mean losing your identity. It's admirable to be a part of an effort, but you do not have to take care of every detail, nor treat everyone with fur gloves. Be peaceful, but not at the expense of your sanity. Be yourself and recognize that you do not have to depend on others to make decisions for your peace of mind or self-esteem like adaptive, caring, and supportive individuals.

Automotive

Youth:

As a baby, the yearning that the number 2 child feels is to be at peace, to be friendly and happy. When rebuked, this child is bored more than expected. The disharmony of any kind can cause the individual to almost cry. When the child is surrounded by questioning authorities, as non-sympathetic brothers, and is the target of unjust criticism, his school and social behavior will suffer.

The young number 2 wants to give and receive love, care, and consideration. For parents, a number 2 child can be "gentle, placid and affable." These are words that describe the individual when surrounded by flexible, soft, and patient authorities.

The young number 2 wants to be appreciated for the little things he does. A supportive position from which you can be prudent, courteous, and diplomatic will leave you at ease. The individual can warm up with the reflected glory of leaders and authorities, for example, and is adaptable and tolerant when involved in group activities. Still, music and rhythm are in your soul, and dance and music lessons—zeal or horn—can prepare you to associate with equals in cooperative adventures in which you can shine.

Maturity:

2 adults want friends, unpretentious love, and comfort. Surround yourself with people who need them because they prefer to do things for others. Rigorous schedules, strict orders, and demanding authorities cause them discomfort. These individuals like to exchange confidences with close friends. The 2 are confident—quiet, helpful, hear the problems.

Aggressive (and corrosive) friends, employers, and companions are attracted to self-motivating people number 2 because the modest 2 do not constitute a threat to leadership, position, and power ambitions. The 2 do not object to forming a support system for more affirmative and dominant friends and colleagues. In their subtle form, the two can impose their points of view. They get what they want and attract recognition for being the amalgam of marriages, families, and business.

The balanced 2 divide or receive credit and recognition with humility. They are, in general, very grateful for small favors and are pleased to reciprocate. Controlling leaders, however, can intimidate them. In the effort to meet demands, they can exhaust their energy. The 2 are well able to deny themselves for the benefit of others.

Self-Image

Youth:

When lying in bed, listening to music and imagining, "How will I be when I grow up? How do I walk, dress, and talk?" The preadolescent number 2 sees himself as a supportive individual. He dreams of a perfect marriage in which, without ties, he helps his partner, and the couple, nestled in a peaceful atmosphere, cautiously climbs the ladder towards comfort and happiness. The number 2 is seen as well-maintained, safe, and cozy.

Children with self-image number two find themselves partners, group leaders, and diplomats. They can solve domestic disputes between siblings and parents, can learn to sew or iron, and get delighted with little treasures that accumulate and grow.

Maturity:

Upon leaving the elevator or entering a room—before the intellect or personality take action—adults number 2 emit prudent and unpretentious vibrations. Their attitude indicates courtesy, and they have a refined and paced look. They tend to subjugate themselves to dress fashions and neutral tones. In order not to be individualistic, the 2s are noted for their elegance and their care with details and accessories.

Self-Expression

Youth:

Adults find it obvious when a child has self-expression number 2. In youth, the number 2 talents are based on the ability to support. The young follow the leader during the jokes. As they grow older, they find that they do not feel comfortable attracting attention. They may decline to make suggestions and be intimidated in the situations that make them stand out.

When teens or young adults, the 2 are good students, they have the talent to be diplomatic, detailed, and skillful organizers. Dance and music classes are good for their artistic skills, and group activities provide them with comfortable recognition. These supportive young people will relate their talents to the instigations, leadership, and creative ideas of family, friends, and authorities.

Maturity:

Suggested Occupations: Secretary, professor, diplomat, accounting technician, accountant, librarian, statistician, biographer, bacteriologist, politician, civil servant, poet, columnist, technical writer, novelist, editor, group singer, group dancer, musician, etc.

The number 2 talents must recognize their own need and desire for harmony and time to carefully perform their tasks. In a work environment, they should set aside emotional judgments and not allow sensitive reactions to color their attitudes. The 2s are concerned about the opinion of others. Balanced number 2 talents prefer to team up with partners and engage in jobs where minutiae are essential and gentle persuasion rather than command. Generally friendly, quiet, and reserved at work, these individuals may choose roles that allow them to interact, one at a time, with individual executives and/or groups.

Destiny:

For this number, achieving harmony is the ultimate goal. Attaining balance is important to allow for a fulfilling life. It is important to strike a balance between both negative and positive traits. While there is nothing wrong with focusing primarily on positive traits, no one is ever perfect. So, using positive traits to offset the negative as much as possible. Once balance is achieved, number 2s find a happy and fulfilling life.

Personal Year

Year 2 is the second year of the nine-year cycle of experience and results in the accuracy and qualification of performance based on the goals set in the first year. It is time to let the experiences recently instigated in the previous year solidify. During the personal year number 2, it is possible to discover who the true friends are and how to be a true friend to others. It's better to play the Mona Lisa and smile mysteriously than to let the little annoyances cause more divisions. Money comes to the hills, small problems come to fruition, and delays can irritate. Personal year number 2 is an occasion to observe, refine, and be willing to take on the responsibility of keeping the peace. Nothing new begins, but you need to maintain friendly relationships with the people who will be around for the next seven years.

Personal Month

The personal month number 2 in the personal year offers the opportunity to make others happy. Interactions with friends and lovers are a top priority, and ambitious material changes must be postponed. The previous month was laborious and tiring, and now it's time to rest and give your close friends time to digest and adjust to things that may be different from your desires. With an open mind, listen to insinuations and constructive criticisms that may be helpful: be kind, adaptable, and understanding in the face of events.

Personal Day

Wake up with a favorable attitude. Whether going to the office or going for a day out, go slow, watching, and feeling the weather. Use intuition when engaging with others. Responding to the needs of others will keep things in peace. Be generous, understanding, and helpful. In return, expect to receive the assistance of family and co-workers today. Do not panic; the time is not propitious to force results.

Accept everything that happens today and have faith that there will be future benefits if you do not change plans or relationships. This day has a purpose: it must be used to support yesterday's activities, absorb information, and reaffirm alliances.

Chapter 7: Number 3 – Communication

Attributes

Positive – Optimistic, imaginative, talented, sociable, Fun, Good Taste, happy, Talkative, Young, Friendly, Greedy

Negative – Disjointed, Complainant, Quirky, Superficial, Tattletale, Narcissistic, Defeated, Distanced, Liar, humdrum

Correspondents

LETTERS: C, L, U

NUMBERS: 12, 21, 30, 39, 48, 57, 66, 75, 84, 93, 102

COLOR: Yellow Yolk

CRYSTAL: Topaz, Galena

VEGETATION: Narcissus-Of-Meadows, Honeysuckle, Orchid, Pink, Pansy, Elm, Mahogany, Sequoia Sempervirens

FOOD: Romaine, Duck, Potato, Tomato, Pudding, Grapes

INSTRUMENTS/PLEA MUSICAL: Bugle, Trombone, Band

MUSICAL NOTE: Mi (When tuning: F

PLANET: Jupiter

MONTHS: March and December

DAYS OF BIRTH: 3, 12, 21, 30

DAY OF WEEK: Thursday

NUMBER OF GENERAL COMPATIBILITIES: 1, 3, 5, 6 (9, business plan

INCOMPATIBILITY NUMBERS: 4, 7 (8, commercial

Challenges of the Number 3

This is a challenge to the individual's communication skills, imagination, and sociability. In particular, the mother and siblings together, or the grandmother and the mother as a whole, either made a lot of fun of the child or put him to bed. The young number 3 is often an only child, boy or girl, the eldest or the youngest in the family. As the preferred or neglected child, challenge 3 becomes a self-aware adult on the social plane, not understanding what he or she has for others. He is incapable of seeing beyond superficial judgments and maturing elegantly. Challenge number 3 can provide superior talent for warmth, humor, artistic expression, and optimism, or the tendency to be intolerant, cynical, spendthrift, or pessimistic. Be that as it may, the 3 are born communicators; they can light a room when they express joy or cause everyone to feel uneasy when they experience sadness. When teens, the 3 or make real scandals with the fall of a hat, or they remain silent. They are extravagant, whether they be heroes or losers. Married, they are jealous or indifferent. When the problems caused by their jealousy become very painful, the 3 simulate alienation. As adults, the 3 perceive friendship as the key that opens the door to love—or else they never reveal themselves or make any commitment to build an alliance. They trust too much—they accept words, gestures, and people without feeling the underlying factors—or, suspiciously, refuse to accept anything by appearance.

Physical Challenges of the Number 3:

This number is with specific physical ailments mainly associated with the upper back and shoulders. These ailments generally come in the form of pain and discomfort resulting from "shouldering the burden." Here are some other physical ailments which may affect number 3s:

- Upper back pain
- Shoulder discomfort
- Neck stiffness
- Migraines
- Sore throat (prone to infection)
- Eyesight (sharpness deteriorating over time)
- Bad posture (especially in taller individuals)

Balancing the challenges of the Number 3

Number 3s are characterized by being sensitive. This is why having outlets that can help 3s manage their feelings is essential. These can come in the way of sports or arts. It really doesn't matter what type of outlet it is so long as it allows 3s to express their feelings in such a way that it becomes constructive rather than destructive.

Also, physical ailments can be improved by allowing 3s to let their feelings out, either by talking about them or simply expressing them creatively. In addition, 3s are sensitive to the pain of others. So, don't be surprised if you, as a 3, end up feeling discomfort due to the empathy you have developed for another person.

Self-Image

Youth:

The talents of number 3 are based on friendliness, imagination, and artistic penchant. As they grow older, the number 3 learns they can talk, dramatize, and pound to get rid of either the practical work or the related responsibilities. When frustrated, they may seem very spoiled, foolish, or theatrical. As charming, customizable, trustworthy little critters, it is difficult for them to suppress their imagination or to stall the chatter.

Without wishing to lie, dramatic number 3 can alter the facts, imitate, or make a scene. 3 strive to be attractive or more interesting. The talents of number 3 place the child in the light of the reflectors. As adults, they will have a more fertile mind, be more educated, and have a better taste if encouraged to verbalize, paint, play an instrument, dance, or write.

Maturity:

Suggested Occupations: Writing—and all means of self-expression that focus on the word. Master of ceremonies, model, actor, designer, artist, musician, singer, salesman, decorator, lecturer, dressmaker, jeweler, social secretary, buyer, bookseller, telephonist, gift wrapper, evangelist, account executive, event promoter, defense or prosecution lawyer, pharmacist, cartoonist, comedian, etc.

Self-Expression

Youth:

Communication is a challenge for 3s when they are young. They may have some trouble with expressing themselves effectively though they may attempt to express it in other ways. As a result, young 3s will endeavor in any number of creative and artistic tasks. If care is taken to foster these talents, older 3s will have no trouble handling their communication skills and expressing their emotions. If left unattended, younger 3s will have a hard time relating to others. These are individuals who might be termed as having "little emotional intelligence."

Maturity:

As 3s get older, their communication skills become paramount to expressing their feelings and ideas. This is very important as 3s who cannot fully express themselves will find it virtually impossible to connect with others simply because they cannot relate with others on a more personal level. This may lead to trouble forming deeper and more meaningful relationships. Communicative 3s can provide tremendous insight and offer words of wisdom whenever required.

Destiny:

Number 3s are meant to be communicators by nature. When 3s develop their communication skills, they are able to let their skills shine through in their interactions with others. 3s are very competent journalists and writers. They might also enter other fields, such as counseling or social work. In short, any type of job or profession which involves communicating with others is right up number 3's alley.

Personal Year

The number 3 is the third year in the nine-year cycle of experience and results in the accuracy and qualification of performance based on the goals set in the first year. It is time to see the ideas and instigations that began two years ago come to fruition. For most, it's a welcome change from the petty problems, the delays, and the emotional worries of the previous year. It is the year that offers opportunities to enjoy lighter interests and increase social contacts. The personal year 3 requires attention to fashions, novelties, and fantasies. Buy clothes. Decorate your home a little. Create an atmosphere that attracts fun.

Love and happiness come to meet them and to bind them. Telephone and postal contacts should be the focus of activating social and business opportunities along with a year to ease workloads, give yourself time to play, and take a vacation.

Festivals, artistic skills, and lovely people should be the focus. Friends provide access to business, fun, and gifts.

Almost every month is lively except April and August. Old and new relationships should be encouraged. It may be that until October, there are only talks, but the topics discussed will bring functional and material goods the following year. For people with destination 3, this year's opportunities will be unforgettable. However, they should keep the main goals in mind and avoid wasting time and money by exploring and expanding the avenues of self-expression. It's a year of pleasure. The romance can sprout and should be seen with a youthful touch. Colleagues may need to be listened to.

During personal year number 3, contacts will be made that provide social activity or attract responses to creative engagements. Work year number 4, below, will not be focused on activities that are impractical or less constructive. This year has a purpose—to relieve tensions and worries. It provides time to watch the amusements promoted by others and to discover creative methods. The year revisits the interest and understanding of the possible joys of feeling in relationships with other people. It sows humor and reminds us that life can be beautiful.

Personal Month

Personal month number 3 in any personal year gives the individual the opportunity to feel unconcerned, lively, and self-expressive. Joyful companions, parties, and all forms of communication are important now. This is no time to pout and stay indoors. After the brakes of the previous month, enjoy this to get out, be seen and heard. The projects started two months ago will now flourish. It's time to tell others about them. Situations will arise that require an attractive appearance and happy physiognomy. Look for old friends. Make a note of someone's phone number at a party, and be sure to call to make a new account. Buy clothes and decorative items for the home. Be prepared to entertain and be entertained. Use this month to verbalize ideas, display talents, and have fun interacting with friends and loved ones.

Personal Day

Wake up with a happy, lively, and friendly attitude. Whether going to the office or going for a day out, chant a melodious song on the way. Invite a friend over for dinner or wait to be invited. Make this day cheerful, and keep an upbeat attitude. Work can seem like a joke and, if that's the case, your mental picture will be contagious. Spread the good news or a joke and dress yourself to attract attention. Hold onto the fun and give others the pleasure of your company.
You may see a lot of talks and little action. This is the day that sets the stage for tomorrow's self-discipline and practical approach. Use this day to make someone smile. Do not let fatalists and those who spread sorrows crush anyone's spirit. Now there is time for hobbies and conversations. Go to the theatre. Play with children and pets. Curl up with a humorous lover and enjoy a good laugh. Loosen up the routines and relax the material goals. Take the initiative to pick up the phone and make time to listen and respond. Above all, go for the sun, and avoid talking about personal problems and anxieties.

Savor what comes today with a pinch of salt and realize that what may seem too worrying is a superficial thing. It will not come true. Certain conversations will involve projects that require practical planning opportunities in the future. This busy day should be used to relax, play, and exchange ideas with positive thinkers.

Chapter 8: Number 4 – Practicality

Attributes

Positive – Practical, Disciplined, Loyal, Organized, Ordered, Factual, Franco, Constructive, Cautious.

Negative – Unproductive, Incompetent, Negligent, Inflexible, Careless, Coarse, Miserly, Rigid.

Correspondents

LETTERS: D, M, V

NUMBERS: 13, 22, 31, 40, 49, 58, 67, 76, 85, 94, 103

COLOR: Green

GEMS: Emerald, Green Jade

CRYSTAL: Cassiterite

VEGETATION: Pepper, Pepper, Pod

FOOD: Grapefruit, Oysters, Veal, Ham, Cod, Yam, Carrot, Pie Morangas, Strawberries, Pretzels, Honey, Coffee.

INSTRUMENTS/MUSICAL APPEAL: Violin, Guitar, Lute; Instrumental.

MUSICAL NOTE: F sharp

PLANET: Uranus

MONTH: April

DAYS OF BIRTH: 4, 13, 22, 31

DAY OF THE WEEK: Sunday

NUMBERS OF GENERAL COMPATIBILITY: 2, 6, 8

INCOMPATIBILITY NUMBERS: 3, 5, 7, 9

Note: If the subject has challenge number 4, these descriptions go from positive to negative until the challenge is balanced. Make sure you read the meaning of the challenge.

Challenges of the Number 4

This is a challenge to the individual's attention to traditions, organizational skills, and the understanding of practical realities. The child often lacked contact with people who were attentive to their needs. Parents strove to provide the child with routine, exteriorities, and appropriate parenting—or else the child's environment lacked conventional planning, practical needs, and stability.

Consequently, the child becomes an extremely organized, self-disciplined, and conservative adult—or else slow to work, careless, and unchanging.

The child may have learned to go to the bathroom with a whip. Schedules and specificities were detailed by the authorities even before the 4 had the emotional or physical ability to meet those requirements. Or the number 4 may not have repeated many routines, and authorities may not have expected great accomplishments or instilled in it the importance of meeting schedules. Either extreme causes frustration in the child and leads him to seek ways to plan and structure the future. The child either develops preventive methods and controls or else abhors the systems.

As an adult, the 4 often focuses too much on the details and the system. They plan and schematize everything and find it difficult to produce something without maximum dedication. Parents of 4, when working, given the need to match children and work, often choose parochial or military schools for ideal secondary learning. If these children are individualistic, creative, and imaginative, these rigid educational systems could make them feel like a fish out of water. On the contrary, if they are spared the quince stick and disciplinary standards, they may not learn that leadership and art also require concentration and discipline. Those with challenge 4 or there are too many rules or shortages, limiting their ability to be flexible or inflexible when there is a practical need to do so. Challenge number 4 can swing from one to the other of the following extremes until the behavior of the challenge bearer is recognized and new habits have been initiated that update their practical self-assessments.

- Very disciplined or very sly.

- Very austere or very informal.
- Very effective or very limited.
- Very practical or very impractical.
- Very economical or very wasteful.
- Very managerial or very unprepared.
- Very perfectionist or very careless.
- Too stiff or too loose.
- Very puritanical or very malicious.
- Very stubborn or very flexible.
- Very ritualistic or very random.
- Too lazy or too busy.
- Very intolerant of very open.
- Very repressed or very free.

Physical Challenges of the Number 4

This list of illnesses and negative habits relates to the challenge of number 4.

- Hypoglycemia
- Blood Problems
- Insomnia
- Vehicle Sickness
- Jaundice
- Cataract
- Liver Problems
- Cystitis

- Migraines
- Foot Puncture
- Rickets
- Gastrointestinal Problems
- Genital Herpes
- Dental Problems
- Halitosis
- Sucking Fingers

Balancing the Challenges of the number 4

The first step in balancing the challenge is to feel free to say, "I need security." Ignore any approach too serious or too free. Use only the restrictions that make it possible for you to live today, and when planning, imagine that you will live 1,000 years. It's your choice. Listen to your feelings. Embrace a friend. Try to relax—who knows!

Dedicate yourself to a sensitive workload and schedule. Work five days a week and save the weekends for fun. Make commitments, make a daily plan, and control the trade and social constraints. You can maintain a slow but steady lifestyle that will give you long-term security. Spend money on necessities and save for the pleasures.

Automotive

Youth:

When reprimanded, they will try to find the rule or routine that will give them back firmness. These babies need direct instruction and discipline. The young number 4 is conformed, conscientious, and serious. When surrounded by disorganized authorities, they will be negligent or stubborn. Parents can describe child number 4 as trustworthy, determined, and methodical, words that describe the individual when surrounded by controlled, sober, and trustworthy authorities.

The four have a legitimate interest in preserving conventions and traditions. As they are very proper, exaggerated displays of love and intimacy may not appeal to them. They love respect, regularity, and unpretentiousness. Family, community, and national pride win loyalty. However, too much self-discipline can be problematic at maturity if these children do not receive affection and affection.

Maturity:

The number 4 adults want to be deliberate, efficient, and trustworthy. They need to structure and steer tasks or goals diligently and feel safe, constant, and convenient. This posture seems somewhat inflexible and resistant to novelties, and it is. They are capable of intense self-sacrifice and feel that without the principles of commitment, stability is an impossible dream.

The number 4 people do not like to be rude or mischievous. Rarely ill-educated or rude friends and lovers need to know what is expected of them in order to satisfy the desires of others. The 4 must receive outlined tasks, and every trustworthy convention, every leader they can rely on, and every practical tool will command their attention. The 4 want material goals and feel more comfortable with people who work to meet traditional needs and help them plan the future. One problem with self-motivation number 4 is the fear of changing routines. They think that loosening them will cause confusion, problems, and loss of control.

Self-Image

Youth:

Lying in bed, listening to music, and thinking, "How will I be when I grow up?" The number 4 is seen as a safe citizen. They dream of leading orderly, respected, and savored lives. The boys see themselves as national protectors, receiving from the country the highest honors for the fulfillment of duty. The girls find themselves diligent owners of a white house with a green lawn, well-protected with the traditional fence of pointy stakes. Children with self-image number 4 see themselves as diligent, dignified, and orderly.

When young, the 4 do not care about trends, news, or fleeting fashions. When surrounded by vibrant and enthusiastic equals, they may seem slow or demanding. Their dream is to control the people and the situations they encounter, because people who are susceptible to be instigated do not make them comfortable, and dodge when they are hurried or undecided. Self-Image number 4 indicates a sturdy body and majestic presence.

Maturity:

As they step out of the elevator or into a room—before the personality or intellect comes into action—the number 4 adults emit carefully upright and conservative vibrations. Their attitude indicates personality with business characteristics, and they seem controlled and attentive. The first impression they give is dependable and sometimes rustic.

Adults that are number 4 become administrators. When they live according to self-image, the first impression implies a failure to solve practical problems. The number of self-expression can govern the first impression as long as formal, fleeting, or extravagant dress codes are indicated in the functional descriptions of the meaning of the number. However, when 4s live according to the self-image, they do not display the corresponding colors indicated by a number in another part of their numerological map.

Self-Expression

Youth:

As they grow up, the 4 discover that they can follow instructions, prepare for activities, and fabricate or fix things to be recognized. When frustrated, they can be servile, insensitive, and resist routines. These helpful, thoughtful, serious, and systematic people feel happier when contributing to a family project. It is difficult not to be stunned by the unyielding practical energy of the 4.

When teens or young adults, the 4 conserve established a routine and focus on things that require personal attention to detail. These teens are not social butterflies or intellectual magicians. They are planners, maintainers, and natural producers of useful products or materials. The 4 need and go to work to obtain material goods. Carpentry, auto mechanics, embroidery, and sewing can keep them occupied. They are not idle and will study, play some sport or find work after school.

Maturity:

As number 4s reach maturity, their logical and organized nature makes the ideal planners. They are organized folks and need to figure everything out before the endeavor into any kind of activity. In some extreme cases, this may lead to inaction because they are chronically hesitant about carrying something out. In the best of cases, they have the foresight and the vision to conduct some of the biggest and most ambitious projects.

Destiny

Since 4s are great at planning, carrying out structured projects, and following instructions, any job such as construction, development, and even real estate brokerage are ideal professions. Also, ambitious endeavors that require a great deal of thought and careful attention to detail may suit 4s well. Project engineers, software developers, and researchers are often very competent number 4s.

Personal Year

The number 4 is the fourth in the nine-year cycle of experiences and results in the hassle and qualification of performance based on the goals set in the first year. It's time to work and let the variety of interests and friendships of the previous year bring social activity. For most, this is a year to correct material mistakes made in the last three years. For others, the year focuses on giving and receiving orders, controlling impulsiveness, and paying attention to a basic routine and a work schedule. And a year of persevering, saving, and accumulating assets. The projects started three years ago.

Self-discipline, restraint, and endurance will be required to make the most of the options open this year. Careful planning, awareness, and efficient attitude are fundamental needs after the dispersion of the previous year. Keywords for this year are caution, dignity, and order. People who volunteer for growth partners this year are not creative, romantic, or open-minded. They are creeping, practical, do not like apathy, incompetence, or frivolity. Faith and trust will have their rewards, and dedication to work will, in addition, attract solidarity. And a year to be sound and rational to correct misconceptions and cultivate long-term goals.

It is necessary to abstain from holidays, festive times, and unscheduled expenses. And you must be attentive to future gratifications. This is the year to buy a new home, repair the old house's roof, or invest in another property. To make the most of this year, you need to be patient, serene, and practical. The systematic approach to day-to-day details and appointments is a must. Do not allow yourself to be constrained by physical responsibilities and demands. Identify the opportunities to put your subjects and your body in functional order. For example, get ready to take advantage of holidays, sexual pleasures, and the chance to break the routine, which is offered the following year in personal year number 5. Get ready to savor freedom, change, and adventure, economizing and acting constructively at this time.

Personal Month

Personal month number 4 in any personal year gives the individual the opportunity to produce tangible results. Serious dedication to economics, routines, and physical fitness should be a top priority. Laziness, disorganization, and impracticality must be pushed back. The previous month did not include responsibilities, and there was time for friends, but now it's time to rebuild plans and projects, as well as set financial and judgmental mistakes. Situations that require a direct approach may arise. Use the occasion to be realistic.

Personal Day

Wake up early and organize plans with a determined attitude. Re-evaluate the details and get rid of mundane tasks. Control the impulses and keep the schedules. Be true to your goals. Use patience, perseverance, and judicious judgment to put the house, work, and social obligations in order. Do not be innovative or mutant. Follow the procedures, count on yourself, and retain dignity. This is no time to experiment or be lazy. Plans for tomorrow, made today, are likely to be changed or canceled, so deal with the details that might restrict tomorrow's freedoms.

Make a personal commitment to persevere until things are done. Let the momentary needs guide the acts of today. Use sweat and planning and do what needs to be done to maintain conventions, discipline, and durability. Be frank and obedient in dealing with superiors; keep your composure, and be reasonable.

Chapter 9: Number 5 – Sexual Freedom

Attributes

Positive – Entrepreneur, Enthusiastic, Operative, Versatile, Intelligent, Lover of Freedom, Fertile, Sensual, Adventurous.

Negative – Irresponsible, Impetuous, Disapproved, Forgotten, Very sexualized, Not objective, Very indulgent, Monotonous, Old-fashioned

Correspondents

LYRICS: E, N, W

DISPOSITION: Sensual, Spontaneous, Inconvenient

NUMBERS: 14, 23, 41, 50, 59, 68, 77, 86, 95, 104

COLOR: Turquoise

GEM: Turquoise Aquamarine

CRYSTALS: white mica, hornblende

VEGETATION: carnation, gardenia, spring

FOODS: Lettuce, celery, cucumber, endive, beets, broccoli, apple, Cherry, Raspberry, Melon

INSTRUMENTS: Bells, Trumpet, Viola

MUSICAL NOTE: SOL (when challenged, G

PLANET: Mercury

MONTH: May

DAYS BIRTH: 5, 14, 23

DAY OF THE WEEK: Wednesday

GENERAL COMPATIBILITY NUMBERS: 1, 3, 7, 9

INCOMPATIBILITY NUMBERS: 2, 4, 6 (8, commercial

Note: If an individual has the challenge of number 5, these descriptions will range from positive to negative until the challenge is balanced. Please be sure to read the meaning of the number of the code.

Challenges of the Number 5

It is a challenge to the individual's understanding of the physical aspects of life. It deals with freedom, indifference, and sexuality. As children, those facing the challenge are exposed to too much or too little loyalty. They do not learn when to join or when to change. Very confusing experiences tax the baby's adaptability, or else it is the adult's caution that binds them too much. This challenge is centered on people's expectations of pleasure and pain, which have been influenced by too much curiosity or insufficient questions.

The number 5 challenge is attracted to sensitive, traditional, and dependable people—or vice versa. They think that everyone who is different from them is interesting. Relationships are usually fleeting, or they drag painfully, and as soon as they understand a person or situation, they tend to be bored. Because of a confused sense of loyalty, the challenged are content to be dispassionate or, then, enthusiastically discover a new interest.

As children, they may have witnessed very quick decision-making. As adults, they risk guesses, or else they investigate carefully before joining a new situation. It is difficult for the challenged to feel who is worthy of their devotion. Your intuitive talent for knowing when to change or what to change has been atrophied. Although immediate diagnosticians of others, the No. 5 challenge cannot spontaneously do what is right for themselves.

Challenge 5 can swing from one to the other of the following extremes until the behavior of the challenge bearer is recognized and new habits that stabilize his or her idleness, curiosity, and sensuality begin.

- Very free or very chained.
- Very versatile or very maladaptive.
- Very satisfied or very unhappy.
- Very irresponsible, or very careful.
- Very understanding or very evil.
- Very excitable or very calm.

- Very adaptable or very firm.
- Very curious or very inert.
- Very smart or very slow.
- Very loyal or very fickle.
- Very sensual or very cerebral.
- Too busy or too bored.
- Very impatient or very serene.
- Very lucky or very unlucky.

Physical Challenges of the Number 5

This list of negative illnesses and habits relates to the challenge of number 5.

- Abortions
- Gum Problems
- Abscesses
- Hemorrhoids
- Accidents
- Infections
- Acne
- Anxiety Problems
- Arthritis
- Multiple Sclerosis
- Brain Tumor
- Obesity

Balancing The Challenge Of Number 5

The first step in balancing the challenge is to feel free to say, "I need to be free." Hold on to a materially productive purpose. Forget the inconsistencies or the unconvincing disappointments of childhood, and remember that you are adaptable. Use the mind to observe, learn, and explore. Stick to a person or job until you get to the details and gain experience. Show your enthusiasm to less curious souls because you have the ability to be a catalyst for change in the lives of others. See people from other angles, stimulate new relationships, and let them evolve.

See yourself as an enthusiastic wildflower, versatile and adaptable, while recognizing that your attitude can make you feel like a weed. But always remember that a weed is a flower that is in the wrong place. Cate carefully your flower beds!

Automotive

Youth:

As a child, the number 5 momentum these children feel is that they are curious, active, and free from restraints. When reprimanded, they become bored or moody. Children number 5 need to apply their enthusiasm and energy in a stimulating way mentally and physically. These young people are discontented, impatient, and daring. Therefore, when surrounded by pragmatic authorities, fixed in routine and solemn, they will be unpredictable or wild. The 5 want progressive, imaginative, and open-minded leadership.

Sports, student politics, journalism, science, and the arts, in the mind of teenager number 5, can today occupy the first place, and tomorrow, the second. A member of the opposite sex can be your rival if you aim for supremacy by using other interests. The 5th may be the male or the sexual muse of the class. An adventure on horseback, on a motorcycle, or challenging the great open space can increase your reserve of life experiences. 5 has a continual impulse to move from some fascinating unknown to another and rarely relaxes its need for expansion.

Maturity:

Adults 5 want to stay young, thought-provoking and moving. The 5 are entrepreneurs who need to find exits to their curiosity and use their enthusiasm to inspire others to experience unfamiliar directions or probe the depths. They want to feel unimpeded, free of responsibility, with an open mind, and a little inconvenience. If this seems unconventional, it is, just as they are. The 5 are often catalysts for changes in the lives of others. They try everything new to themselves and take advantage of speculation.

One problem with self-motivation number 5 is the fear of being tied up. They think that if they settle conventionally, their style will be atrophied. Business, social, intimate, and family relationships must adapt to their rapid cadence and mutant ideas. Over time, various people and experiences excite their fantasies. They retain anything or anyone that cannot be assimilated or schematized and easily forget the unpleasant experiences. The balanced 5 live the now.

Self-Image

Youth:

Lying in bed, listening to music, and thinking, "How will I be when I grow up? How am I going to walk, dress, and talk?" Young numbers 5 look like deranged demons. They dream of leading a life without hindrance, of discoveries at random and unconventional. The boys see themselves winning the biggest lottery prize in the country and spending it all on pleasures. Girls find themselves traveling the world, meeting mythical people, and directing attention to wherever it takes them the pleasure of wandering. Self-image children can see themselves as uninhibited adventurers, fearless, and provocative sex symbols.

Young people whose dreams are based on the meaning of number 5 can be too adventurous and create confusion. They affirm themselves to have freedom of choice and action. Their joint aspect is out of the ordinary: they are to stop the traffic.

Maturity:

When exiting the elevator or entering a room—before personality or intellect comes into action—the adult number 5 emits provocative, non-traditional, and sociable vibration. His attitude indicates a vibrant personality, and seems willing to everything. The first impression she gives is energetic, sometimes lively, and always determined. If self-expression and self-expression numbers are introverted or conventional, the 5 look well-groomed and colorful. Dress styles, posture, and attitude do not necessarily indicate their sensual or adventurous self-image.

Self-Expression

Youth:

When they grow up, the 5 do not follow instructions, do not stand still, or accept rigid routines. To dodge problems, they seduce disciplinarians and teachers. They are helping people, fertile in solutions and gossip, eager to add enthusiasm to family projects. It's hard not to be surprised by their intelligence, inventiveness, and adaptability.

Maturity:

A mature 5 is all about achieving ultimate self-expression. From the experience that they have accumulated over the years, they can better express their wishes and desires. They allow them to have a greater degree of freedom and liberation. They can embrace who they are and make the most of the time ahead of them. Many 5s have gotten a grip on their sexuality regardless of what their orientation might be. They have reached a point in their lives where they are comfortable with being who they are.

However, 5s who have not come to grips with who they are will struggle to find a balance in their later years. These may lead to feelings of bitterness and resentment, particularly if they feel sexually unsatisfied. It is important to note that they may find other ways of liberating this type of pent up energy though they may still feel frustrated or unfulfilled to a certain extent.

Destiny

5s tend to be extroverted and outgoing. They enjoy being in the spotlight and in contact with people. They are great at getting along with other people. The service industry is the first stop for 5s. Here are some suggested occupations: Actor, lecturer, writer, theatrical producer, promoter of events, advertising, street vendor, public relations specialist, reservations agent, politician, advertising consultant, lawyer, psychologist, director of personnel, engineer-designer, inventor investigator, detective, insurance inspector, newspaper reporter, among others.

Personal Year

The number 5 is the fifth in the nine-year cycle of experience that results in the accuracy and qualification of performance based on the goals set in the first year. It's time to get away from the routines, keeping in mind the practical assessments of the previous year when it may come with sexual pleasures and transitions. For the most part, it is a time of rapid cadence—filled with people and new scenarios—aimed at sowing curiosity, adding versatility, resulting in a broader perspective. For the others, the year focuses on accommodating an indoctrination that began in October of the previous year. It's an energetic year to learn from experience, discard old ideas, and think about seeing long-term goals from a different angle. It is necessary to keep in mind the material ambitions in risking a new approach to business, home, and lifestyle.

You have to risk the unknowns and not be afraid to make spontaneous decisions. It is not a year to buy a home or assume new responsibilities. To make the most of this year, we must relieve the obligations of daily work and eliminate practical and emotional hindrances. The voluntary, vigorous, and original approach to the many possibilities offered should make this a lively year.

Year 5 will test the individual's ability to feel free, at ease, and yet remain constructive. Understand that progress depends on tolerance and taking advantage of new experiences and does not anticipate the end result or prejudge how people will interact. The attitude is very significant: it is better to swim in favor of the tide.

Personal Month

Personal month number 5 in any one year personal provides the opportunity to make transitions and changes. Extravagant ideas, travel, and the drive to reduce responsibility should have top priority. Narrow views, stiffness, and continued efforts should be put aside. The previous month was filled with realities and practical limitations, and there was little time for experimentation. Now is the time to risk love and luck. Enjoy the excitement, the new people, and the opportunities that open up. Situations may arise that require a premonition. Use this month to be an entrepreneur: try something different, something that attracts attention, and be spontaneous. Be flexible, enterprising, and keep your mind open when faced with unexpected possibilities.

Personal Day

Wake up sooner or later and openly address the unconventional opportunities of every hour. Whether going to the office, for a day off, or to the grocery store, do it differently. Try and change perspectives. Dress to stop the traffic, delay in lunch, and welcome with enthusiasm everything that comes. Be responsible when necessary, but allow yourself to feel indoctrinated, sociable, and sensual. In other words, expect to be flexible. Show everyone that you are the one that is indicated for the yaws, ready to take the direction at the time of change or change of plans. Make a personal decision to do something that the moment instigates. Use the charm, the insight, and the adventurous ideas to disconcert someone, but make room for unprogrammed socialization or chance. Turn to the greater responsibilities of tomorrow, to the conventional obligations and to the priority of emotional relationships, living to regain routines and to make room for commitments.

Chapter 10: Number 6 – Formation

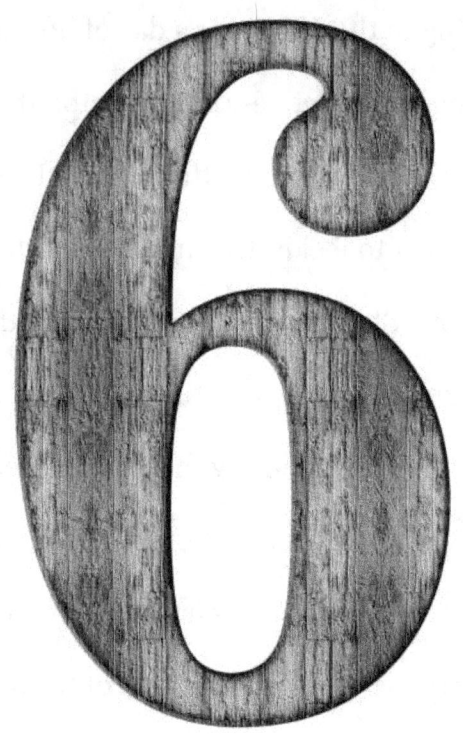

Attributes

Positive – Conscientious, Reliever, Generous, Stable, Dedicated, Idealist, Intelligent, Convenient, Worried about Home.

Negative – Suffocated, Palpation, Worried, Inexorable, Intolerant, Carefree, Unreliable, Martyrized, Discontent.

Correspondents

LETTERS: F, O, X

NUMBERS: 15, 24, 33, 42, 51, 60, 69, 78, 87, 96, 105 COLOR: Blue

GEMSTONES: Sapphire Blue, Pearl White-Blue, Diamond

CRYSTALS: Indicolite (Blue Tourmaline)

VEGETATION: Chrysanthemum, Dandelion, Bay, Tulip, Palm, Poplar, Rosewood.

FOOD: Potatoes, Spaghetti, Sweet potato, Pork, Fish, Siri, Rye bread, Parsley, Orange, Banana, Peach.

INSTRUMENTS/MUSICAL APPEAL: Banjo, Harmonica, Concert, Hymn, Musical.

PLANET: Venus

MONTH: June

DAYS OF BIRTH: 6, 15, 24

DAYS OF THE WEEK: Friday

GENERAL COMPATIBILITY NUMBERS: 2, 3, 4, 9 (8 IN LOVE

INCOMPATIBILITY NUMBERS: 1, 5, 7, 8

Note: When the individual is challenged with the number 6, these descriptions go from positive to negative until the challenge is balanced. Please be sure to read the meaning of the challenge number.

Challenges Of The Number 6

This is the challenge of accountability, obligations to personal relationships, and emotional decisions. It is rooted in too little or insufficient family and community focus in childhood. Parents, siblings, and generations of ancestors may have over-weighed the child's morals, ethics, and standards. There may have been no household responsibility and unity at an early age. The child may have been encouraged to be too mature or, then, to have been heavily protected.

Challenge 6 people may feel selfish when he or she does not feel like taking on loads that are overweight. The adult with this challenge volunteers too much, gives many hunches, and grieves with everything. If the bearer of challenge 6 sacrifices himself too much, he becomes selfish and controversial and feels like a martyr. In these circumstances, he loses his talent for fostering loving, peaceful, and fruitful relationships.

As adults, they seek the needy and are sought after by them. They emit vibrations that stimulate dependency and rebel when they find themselves in bondage. It's the office or leisure club volunteers who teach and help without being asked. But when they take responsibility for a whole project and do more than they can, they feel used. The result is that nobody appreciates it. Overloaded, they inadvertently lead the "users" to feel guilty.

Challenge number 6 can swing from one to the other of the following extremes until the wearer recognizes their behavior and begins new habits that stabilize their opinions.

- Very presumptuous or very insecure.
- Very firm or very weak.
- Very cynical or very loving.
- Very critical or very unconcerned.
- Very anxious or very calm.
- Very concentrated in the family or very lonely.

- Very stubborn or very complacent.
- Very intractable or too tight.
- Very harmonious or very disharmonious.
- Very protective or very suspicious.
- Very concerned or very selfish.
- Very overbearing or very dependent.
- Too worried or too irresponsible. Very paternal or very immature.

Physical Challenges of the Number 6

The list of diseases and negative habits below relates to the challenge of number 6.

- Breast Cyst
- Kidney Problems
- Colitis
- Cramp problems
- Menstrual Problems
- Dental Problems
- Fatigue
- Excess Weight
- Urinating in Pants
- Problems in the Prostate
- Hemophilia
- Stomach Problems

- Ulcer
- Hypertension

Balancing the Challenges of the Number 6

The first step in balancing the challenge is to feel free to say, "I need harmony." Allow close people to take care of their own work, have their own opinions, and take on their own duties. You are not responsible for the family, neighborhood, office employees, community, or the world.

Assume obligations when requested. When you see the need to volunteer, ask the person who needs assistance if she wants your contribution—sometimes, a temporary loan or a minute of your time is enough. Most of the needy open up, but if you feel you are inhibited, ask how you can help them.

Automotive

Youth:

As children, these people experience the impulse of number 6 to feel part of a whole, loving and caring. When rebuked, they try to calm the authorities or act as if they are hurt. These children need comforting relationships emotionally and physically to maintain a peaceful feeling. Young people, number 6, is not likely to start discussions. No, in fact, they do not interfere, they do not complain, and they are affectionate ushers. When surrounded by distant or negligent authorities on the domestic plane, they will be protective and anxious. They want and need compassionate, pertinent, and instructive leadership.

Young ethicists like to promote happiness and friendship and want to heal all mistakes. On the specific plain, poor, and personalistic idealists and artistic people can engage them almost effortlessly. Parents should teach them not to exaggerate their friendliness, for otherwise, after school, they may find the kitchen full of starving schoolchildren, tasting the dinner dessert. Still, disabled colleagues who appeal to the number 6 solidarity can benefit from their impulse to teach.

Maturity:

Adults number 6 want to be determined, trustworthy, and discerning. They need to find exits for good taste and use their understanding, encouraging, and comforting others. In general, they want to feel loved, loved, and respected. If this goal seems a bit conventional, it is, as are the 6. However, the number 6 adults should be able to create stability from irresponsibility. After assessing problems, they are able to direct people's lives. They have sincere impulses to counsel, to do justice, and to follow the errands to the end make them superb therapists, teachers, and nurses.

One problem with self-motivation number 6 is to understand why others need solitude. They think life would be intolerable without social intercourse and a safe place to nest. Because of their close ties to the family, if they even want to be alone once in a while, they cause surprise. In this way, commercial ambitions may exist second to family obligations.

The number 6 is concerned with paying the bills, decorating the house, and making the right impression on loved ones. Your biggest goal is staying in one place and creating the reputation of being trustworthy and interacting with safe, romantic, and considerate people. The six want to love and love with gusto.

Self-Image

Youth:

When lying in bed, listening to music and thinking, "How will I grow up? How will I walk, dress, and talk?" Young people number 6 become homegrown people. They dream of leading a comfortable, hospitable, and responsible life. Boys find themselves in respectable positions in which they provide competent services, comfort others, and provide sustenance for a loving and beloved family. Girls see themselves as friends and companions who are supportive and always present when necessary and are dedicated to marriage or a position of responsibility. Children with self-image number 6 may see affectionate paternal or maternal types who cultivate family ties, manifest artistic interests, and contribute to the community's well-being.

Young people with dreams based on the meaning of number 6 can be self-styled, and by prolonging their emotional solidarity to such an extent, they are often devastated by the attraction they feel for dependent persons. They will do everything they can to correct situations that cause problems for people who love or want to help. They seem able to create harmony in their own lives and the lives of members of their families and community.

Maturity:

When they leave the elevator or enter a room—before the personality or intellect takes action—the number 6 adults emit vigorous, quiet, and comforting vibrations. Their attitude indicates a solitary personality and legitimate solicitude. The first impression of the six is firm, sometimes artistic, and always warm. If the numbers of self-motivation and self-expression are mental or introverted, the number 6 will look quiet and peaceful. Dress styles, posture, and attitude do not reveal their emotional or protective self-image. The number 6 adults are mature. When you live according to your self-image, the first impression you make lets you see the fall to take on the problems of others.

Self-Expression

Youth:

Not to be nosey, supportive number 6 may consciously and obsequiously become very concerned about the problems or affairs of others—the result is that any serious consideration of consideration can lead to complications or confusion. For parents who do not reveal themselves and have entrepreneurial characteristics, the 6 may seem very troublesome, nosy, and embarrassing. On the other hand, for affectionate adults and participants, they are accepted as welcome co-workers of the family. Parents can probably calm these children by giving them more domestic responsibilities.

As teens, these community-minded perfecters often receive positions of responsibility and trust. They are successful diplomats and will try to reorganize or make adjustments whenever they feel that people or things do not meet their standards. The 6 rarely shy away from the engagements and have passionate opinions and dramatic pronouncements that will be heard. When frustrated or hurt by disloyalty, intolerance, or pessimism, they may overeat, lose themselves by working for others or smother pets with affection. They are faithful when they are admired, but when hardened, they may be disgruntled, envious, and case-makers.

Destiny

Number 6s are a mix of passion and creativity. They are also caring and thoughtful. That is why professions and occupations which deal with providing care are high on their radar. Also, 6s are practical and goal-oriented. So, occupations that tend to have clearly defined goals and objectives are also especially appealing. 6s do well as a sociologist, interior decorator, vocational counselor, academic adviser, practical or licensed nurse practitioner, veterinarian, hospital administrator, student, teacher, assistant professor, social worker, costume designer, etc.

Maturity:

The 6 can be rewarded financially for their ability to provide services, assume responsibilities, and be trusted employees and just employers. Still, they can be recognized for their talent of providing comfort, integrity, and dominance of the scene when needed or requested. In particular, they attract positions that require rapport, trustworthiness, and compliance.

Personal Year

The number 6 is the sixth cycle of nine years of experience that results in the accuracy and qualification of performance based on the goals outlined in the first year. It's time to focus on the responsibilities of the home, family, and community. One should keep in mind the freedom of the previous year when April initiates new projects and consciously accommodate loved ones and acquaintances on the occasion of requests. And a receptive period filled with domestic tasks and maintenance obligations. It is better to welcome what appears. "What goes around," and this year, you cannot expect to suffice yourself or receive love without repaying it. This year will have as a center the comfort of others, and personal adjustments should be made to the chronological changes produced in the previous October. And a year in which progress is measured by emotional generosity, and in November, the bread thrown into the waters will return.

The personal year number 6 is called the wedding year. Whether you are marrying a person or a job, your commitments must now be given top priority. One must plan the future, live each day as if it were the last, and not go to bed angry. One must decide to clear the differences at the end of each day and greet the morning, free of hostility. The stripped-down attitude is very significant. Although it is better to expect to be asked, assistance can be provided when necessary. Social activities or trips should be centered on family and community projects, as there are no new directions indicated. It is time to deepen the bonds and preserve the predicates.

Personal Month

Personal month number 6 in any one-year period gives the individual the opportunity to focus on loved ones and home and community responsibilities. Traveling is not advisable unless you are visiting family. Emotional receptivity, improvements, and preservation of peaceful relationships should be given top priority. Intellectual, intolerant, and self-aware views must be put aside. The previous month has given you the chance to get out of the rut, and now it's time to fix yourself, deepen love and create harmony.

Personal Day

Wake up early and address the hourly responsibilities with a demonstration of integrity. Perform each task with determination and awareness. Do not try. Dress to do things and feel comfortable. Be prepared to be held accountable for all the facts and observations, but also remember that this day is to show love and affection by taking on the weak or needy problems. Expect to make personal adjustments when needed, without turning work into a burden. Show the world the lover, partner, or realistic, caring, and supportive friend that you are.
Make a personal commitment to go where you need help. Embrace someone and disconcert people with sincere concern and practical advice. Set aside time for domestic shopping and to visit family or some sick friend. Today is the day to focus on rejoicing others. Delays in tomorrow's communications and reduction of physical energy give you the opportunity to analyze past or future goals and to use personal time for self-evaluation.

Chapter 11: Number 7 – Mental Analysis

Attributes

Positive – Analytical, Authoritarian, Mystical, Meticulous, Introspective, Aristocratic, Logical, Researcher, Wise.

Negative – Offensive, Caustic, Cynical, Coarse, Haughty, Uncouth, Critical, Superficial.

Correspondents

LETTERS: G, P

NUMBERS: 16, 25, 34, 43, 52, 61, 70, 79, 88, 97, 106

COLOR: Purple (Violet)

GEM: Alexandrite (Amethyst)

CRYSTALS: Amethyst, Rutile violet:

VEGETATION: Saffron, Geranium, Marigold, Poppy, Fern

FOODS: Herring, Omelette, Spinach, Roasted Pork, Goose, Blackberry.

INSTRUMENTS/MUSICAL APPEAL: Harp, Ballet

PLANET: Neptune

MONTH: July

DAYS OF BIRTH: 7, 16, 25

DAYS OF THE WEEK: Monday

GENERAL COMPATIBILITY NUMBERS: 7 (Friendship, 5 (Business

INCOMPATIBILITY NUMBERS: 1, 3, 6, 8, 9

Note: When the individual is challenged with the number 7, these descriptions will go from positive to negative until the challenge is balanced. Please be sure to read the meaning of the challenge number.

Challenges of the Number 7

This is the challenge to the individual's ability to accept worldly realities and keep faith in himself. It is rooted in a children's environment that did not recognize the child's intellectual curiosity or that could not finance formal education for them. Parents may have felt socially insecure, or the young man may have intuitively realized that his family or his right to live was surrounded by certain mysteries that should have to do with that little lettering of legal documents. The facts of health, sensibility, or commercials were illusory or nebulous, and emotional responses were rationed. The information ambushed beneath the surface, and for the young man, everything resulted in loneliness, disillusionment, and disgust.

Parents and authorities may have based their values on superficial or commercial achievements, while the child's value system was structured on the grounds of inquiry, quality, and wisdom. The child with challenge number 7 responds to stress by isolating himself into a solitary secret that coherently or reads between the lines or takes everything literally.

In youth, the individual is likely to hamper their relationships because of a reserved, emotionally blank, and critical attitude. As an adult, challenge number 7 must learn to accept others' earth-down, aggressiveness, and openness. You must learn to live in a world where everyone belches, sometimes they eat with the wrong fork, and the average person does not have the patience to seek the hidden truths. As children, individuals with challenge number 7 abandon their goals, become book moths, or tend to join a select intellectual group. They see themselves alone against the vulgar herd. They feel rebellious, secretive, and arrogant when exposed to rude, coarse, or opaque people who do not understand them in a different orbit.

The number 7 challenge bearer holds a secret intruder-proof self and feeds the fear of merging or losing himself in passionate alliances, even if someone has already penetrated his skin and touched his heart. He can marry but, when he tells his secret to the other, he usually does it to the wrong person. He can stifle communication when he acts in a very detached or authoritarian way. They can take refuge in meditation or subtly hide your emotions in material interests. In other words, the 7 can enter into a state of mind that guarantees your privacy.

Until these individuals recognize the desire to improve their circumstances, they may not be absorbed by the quality of life. The 7s balance their challenge when communicating thoughts to acquaintances, develop a sense of material self-worth and have enough faith to follow their intuition. Business evolution will have frustrating beginnings and disruptions until the 7th becomes a specialist or an authority.

Those with this challenge have a unique talent for mental games that suggest extracorporeal experience. Still, in pursuit of perfection, these individuals observe their own acts and behaviors and often think they are the only ones who can criticize.

Lowering guard, forming isolating mannerisms, and abandoning erroneous and self-deprecating ideas is more difficult for the bearer of this challenge than for anyone else. The bearer of this challenge habitually fears the impropriety of solitude and poverty, and his escape resources often leave him helpless, make him his own scarecrow. These and other introspective habits prevent you from engaging in activities outside your own envelope. He is asked to replace imaginary fears and skepticism by faith in himself and in humanity. The challenge of number 7 implies that the individual's disadvantages are self-imposed and unjustified, when, in fact, the 7 is well-endowed intellectually and spiritually.

Challenge number 7 can swing from one to the other of the following extremes until new habits are established that stabilize the repression experienced by its bearer.

- Very critical or very incompetent.

- Very investigative or very opaque.
- Very squeaky or too off.
- Very naive or very skeptical.
- Very authoritarian or very credulous.
- Very secretive or very open.
- Very uncertain or very safe.
- Very bookish or very uncultured.
- Very perceptive or very mystified.
- Very aristocratic or very rude.
- Very patient or very rushed.
- Too deep or too careless.
- Too distant or too greedy.
- Very complex or very simple.
- Too rational or too silly. Too fast or too slow.

Physical Challenges of the Number 7

Challenges can affect physical as well as mental health. Body chemistry changes when individuals are stressed, and when we do not know what is good for us, our minds detonate anxious, angry, or frustrated habits. When we mistreat ourselves, we become sick. The individual's attitude sends a message to the brain, which tells the body to scream for help.

In order to draw attention to their malaise, people often get sick or form negative habits. Numerologists believe that illness and well-being depend on attitude, and challenges indicate attitudes that result from needy feelings. When we do not feel needy, we feel good and balanced and do not beg for the attention of others. Essentially, if the personality challenges are balanced, and the body chemistry is balanced, the risk of mental or physical illness is small.

Challenge numbers indicate the ways in which people punish themselves unconsciously for not being consciously good about themselves.

This list of illnesses and negative habits relates to the challenge of number 7.

- Addiction
- Lumbar Problems
- Adenoid Problems
- Alcoholic Personality
- Allergies
- Anemia
- Arteriosclerosis
- Blood Pressure
- Cysts in Breasts
- Cold
- Cramp
- Unruly Depression
- Diagnostic Difficulty
- Menstrual Problems
- Nausea
- Neck Problems

- Problems in Prostate

Balancing the Challenges of the Number 7

The first step in balancing the challenge is to feel free to say, "I must have faith." Discover an area of concentration in which to deepen and gain experience. Academic credits count, but they are not the only path of specialization.

The best way to build faith in yourself and others is to wake up each morning to a job you love. If you are willing to follow learning or research, and if there are time and integrity invested in your goal, you will be qualified. His talent for accuracy, originality, and research attracts other professionals with good taste and insight. If you make a commitment, you'll find friends among your peers.

To balance this challenge, it is necessary to follow your intuition, first thought, or foreboding. An important part of his special ability is to use his inner resources. Do not be intimidated by titles, politics, or self-promotion. Listen to the advice of well-selected professionals and then do what you feel is best. Remember that you do not have to answer to anyone but yourself; therefore, if there is a conflict between your foreboding and logic, follow your foreboding. You will discover that you are your best friend and guide.

Sadness, melancholy, and flight from reality are habits that can be stopped. When the bearers of this challenge meet goals, people always come to share their thoughts, and mistrust, repression, and denunciations disappear, taking away the stress induced by negativism. Challenge 7 bearers can build faith in humanity when they share their inner insights and capacities. The answer encourages self-confidence, and the resulting changes in personality can be miraculous. Nothing works better here than the combination of sixth sense and common sense. When they fail to expect perfection of themselves and of humanity, the doors open to self-esteem and self-help. The challenge will be mitigated when these individuals realize that perfection can only be found on another cosmic plane. And in that, nobody is perfect!

Automotive

Youth:

For children number 7, the greatest impulse is to be observant, quiet, and questioning. When rebuked, these children become recluses, hide, and cry alone. Young people number 7 are trustworthy, intuitive, and solitary. When surrounded by superficial, gregarious, and overly emotional authorities, they shut them up. They want calm, refined, and rational leadership, and they need toys that stimulate the intellect to satisfy their curious minds.

Parents can describe their number 7 children as deliberate, rational, and studious. These words describe these individuals when they are surrounded by learned, observant, and mature authorities. If the introspective personality of Number 7 is considered odd, and parents disregard their need to meditate, these children may become reticent and reluctant to reveal their thoughts. Young people number 7 want to investigate, read books, and discuss their observations on a technical level—this is when they come to reveal their perceptions. If these children, who have difficulty expressing their feelings, receive affection and love, they become more animated and authoritative. Generally speaking, these young people are secretive, particularly as regards their sensitivity and their emotional reactions. Children with number 7 need permission to create their own world: their innate wisdom must be taken seriously and channeled into mental activities. Going to the library, harp lessons, and opportunities to listen to classical music will be stimuli to your already avid intellects. The 7 acquire knowledge by investigating the topics that interest them. They will not have a large group of friends, nor will they socialize spontaneously, and very few relationships with their peers in their youth can be a problem. Children number 7 are discriminating and prefer solitude to boring companies. By turning to spiritual or intellectual pursuits, quiet, inspiring, or theoretical conversations with older, read people should satisfy any desire they may have for social intercourse. Willing number 7 likes silence, peace, and solitude. These individuals may be at the forefront of the class academically but may be socially immature. The 7 may be shy, self-absorbed, and defensive when with classmates, preferring to ignore retrograde educational procedures, abstain from parties, and invent their own mind games. On the whole, intimacy causes them discomfort.

The 7 are aristocratic loners who become melancholy when surrounded by rudeness and people who push them to materialistic priorities. Surprisingly, they fear loneliness, but they make it difficult to get to know others. When they are sure of the facts surrounding them, and only there, the 7 enter into the conversation. Parents should expose them to the intricacies of photography, computers, and the world of metaphysics to direct their interest and keep them occupied.

Young people with number 7 need to wear cotton shirts, sweaters that do not scream and should be in contact only with the best that exists. Of 10 dresses in the hanger of a store, girl number 7, without the intention of cunning, chooses the most expensive and the best made. When they buy school notebooks, boys automatically choose the most effective and best made. These children feel comfortable with the quality and prefer to satisfy a desire rather than a bunch of commitments.

It is best to teach young people with number 7 early on to accept human frailty and their imperfections. The chatterboxes, the manual labor, and the sports they demand from the physicist do not appeal to them, and they tend to be brainstorming researchers who perceive the world with reservations and think harder before accepting a job. Classical technical, scientific, or academic education will be of great help to these children, and any specialization will be the target for them to feel at ease. The numbers 7 individuals fit into many professional, refined, and reserved groups of people.

The 7s are perfectionists who reach maturity by carefully dissecting every detail of their lives before proceeding. If the 7 have more conventional numerical meanings in other aspects of their maps, they may not be introverts. However, they are likely to find a way to preserve respect for their privacy.

As teenagers, deftly, the 7s do one thing at a time. As adults who seek the truth, they want all the information available before making any decisions. Alert parents understand that these sedentary analysts are indeed listening to the music of the spheres. The number 7 rarely has a sense of urgency or obsession with material goods. They attract money, recognition, and influential alliances as they follow their instincts to question everything.

Maturity:

Number 7 adults want to be purists undisturbed by practical realities or worldly people. They need to be surrounded by timeless treasures and may seem disconnected from the world most of the time. They want to be perceptive, contemplative, and scholarly. Your desires and accomplishments form a category by itself.

People number 7 do not like to surround themselves with busy businesspeople, noisy phones, or cliché typewriters. Lovers seldom gregarious or excited, knowing that they do not need to express constant demonstrations of affection, produce the perfect criteria for the patient soul mate. The 7 do not feel comfortable when they are expected to be obsessed with sensuality or when they are pressured into a demanding social whirlwind. On the other hand, any theoretical discussion, any enlightening television program, or sophisticated recipe leaves us intrigued. When unbalanced, these individuals may want a desperate escape. They may be obsessive fanatics or aggressive dreamers on the commercial plane. When balanced, they are rational, discerning, and conscientious originals. When under the care of number 7, young people learn to be inquiring, meticulous, and resourceful. Capable of following their instincts, the number 7 adults are astute, broad-minded, and proud parents.

You can expect a balanced, resourceful, thoughtful, and patient individual to figure out how to attract things or lovers that fit your expectations. It is very improbable to find balanced self-motivation 7 that is self-satisfied, openly affectionate, and instigated by dramatic means.

Those who have self-motivation number 7 have problems with feelings of introspection, melancholy, and emotional poverty.

They tend to fear their own desire for separatism. The 7 do not like to live quiet, but they cannot be true to themselves in routinely competitive business environments. When they follow the natural instinct to become academics, professionals, and experts, the prospects of financial success are good. In spiritual or metaphysical pursuits, the 7 are attuned to the mastery of the deeper truths, and their discoveries can be extraordinary.

Self-Image

Youth:

When lying in bed, listening to music and thinking, "How will I grow up? How will I walk, dress, and talk?" Young people number 7 become aristocrats. They dream of leading a serene life of quality, free to investigate, select, and analyze. The boys see themselves as authoritarian, lecturing on the favorite specialty for their intellectual peers, and the girls see themselves as the reincarnation of Margaret Mead or Madame Curie, surrounded by silent and serious students in a room of shelves full of bound books or in a laboratory wide and perfect. Children with self-image number 7 may see themselves as proud, dignified, and confident royalty—above the mundane and low-hanging obligations of youth— and are usually called princes or princesses.

The 7 may appear to be self-assured, thoughtful, and quiet children who have the intellectual ability to meddle with their elders. When the number 7 says they want to be scientists, photographers, or priests, they find themselves in the right position to use their erudite, technical, or mystical ideas. When they live according to self-image, these individuals will be the first to read the dish's recipe, following every ingredient and instruction, and criticize the dish after savoring the fruit of the work they attribute to others. These children, these teens or young adults, do not like to get their hands dirty or sweat at work. They seek to avoid mundane work and tend to assume the position of specialists or authorities. Young people with dreams based on the meaning of number 7 may have discriminating tastes. They are difficult to please, and they enforce physical, mental, and spiritual privacy. Its overall appearance is coordinated carefully, with pastels and light materials. They are not inclined to call attention, so they use classic styles instead of affirming fashion. When in tune with self-image, they have a sense of style so harmonious that it impresses, and they dress and dress impeccably.

The 7 rarely seem emotionally expressive or mercenary. The youthful expectations of number 7 are not sensual or materially ambitious. Not; for this haughty self-image, intimate desire is centered on solitary inquiry, analysis, and deductions based on the world above, below, and around you.

Maturity:

When leaving the elevator or entering a room—before the personality or intellect comes into action—the adult with the self-image 7 emits dignified and refined vibration. His attitude indicates a reserved personality and pride. The first impression she makes is serene, sometimes curious, and always of good lineage.

When self-expression and self-expression numbers are outgoing or unconventional, the number 7 uses unique color combinations and looks decidedly fancy.

The number 7 adults perceive themselves to be experts or critics and can be very quick to guess. When they live according to self-image, the first impression can intimidate, and may not relate well to all.

The number of self-expression can govern the first impression as long as practical or flashy costumes are indicated by the vocational descriptions delineated in the meaning of the number. The number of self-motivation can influence the wearer's wear as long as they are relaxed and doing what they want to do. However, when these individuals live by self-image, they will not display corresponding colors or styles indicated by the numbers elsewhere on their numerological map.

Self-Expression

Youth:

Adults find it obvious when children have self-expression number 7 since in youth, the talents 7 are based on questioning everything: in asking why the sky is blue and why birds fly. Because they do not accept superficial explanations and investigate all the answers, the 7 keep the parents mentally alert and send the teachers to the reference library. When they grow up, they research hobbies, read for hours, and enjoy playing or listening to stringed instruments. They leave the authorities perplexed and push away the less introspective equals. Helpful,

Accurate, perceptive, and in search of truth, these children add refinement to the family project. It's hard not to be surprised by their intelligence and meticulousness.

Not wanting to be rude, a logical number 7 can take a thorough and penetrating attitude to rules and regulations. Every original and well-founded criticism must be discussed in a persistent and ingenious way. Flexible, insatiable, and industrious fathers may seem too demanding, pretentious, or shrewd. For educated, calm, and cerebral adults, the instinctive nobility of purpose, intellectual curiosity, and the sincerity of 7 are expected and welcomed. The need to investigate the children, to get to the root of everything, will be respected.

As teenagers, these bookish perfectionists can close themselves in concentration and set impervious to noise, hunger, or fun. Despite their general disregard for light jokes and conventional social interactions, they are capable of eloquent speech or hilarious humor when they are on their whim. New puns, mathematical logic games, cameras, and computers can fascinate them. They are intellectuals and should take every opportunity to use their sharp brains. Museums, ancient ruins, and everything that justify a photograph will give them the opportunity to develop artistic interests. They are not sloppy, disinterested, or amateurish and seek the scientific or technical approach when researching on their own. As observers, number 7s hesitate and do not speak or assume leadership roles without being sure of the facts. They may prefer to be used as accessories, but as soon as they find a professional interest that offers mental challenges, a refined environment, and the opportunity to work independently, the 7 demonstrate to be knowledgeable quality experts.

In their youth, the 7 prefer light fabrics, tasteful clothes, and fine, well-prepared foods. Once they discover the things that work in their favor, they do not make changes. In general, the 7 disregards the novelties, the nonsense, and the dramatic displays of emotion. Feel at ease with non-competitive subjects where you do not need to follow the crowd or dress uniformly. The 7s do not feel comfortable when highlighted, they prefer a lower profile, and ignore the less evolved opinions. They seem to do everything in a hurry, and during crises, they try to control their emotions and act cool.

Children, adolescents, and young people should deserve privacy and be encouraged to see all sides of everything. With books and recognized authorities, they can learn to become scientists, technicians, or leading spiritual leaders.

Maturity:

Self-expression number 7 has the potential to reward itself financially because of the ability to investigate all aspects of a subject, to perfect techniques, and to discover the findings with confidence. It is possible to recognize the superior intuition and talent of number 7 to appreciate or produce quality work. The 7 draw positions that require specialized information and in which sharp perception is convenient. Your communications are deliberate, precise, and logical. These researchers are sincere, patient, and undisturbed. The 7 become the center of attention when they probe an idea and prove its worth.

Innate mystical talents often make researchers look eccentric. They should seek wisdom without forgetting worldly needs, financial stability, and domestic responsibilities. Mental explorations and fascination with spirituality and para-sciences often prevent the innate parapsychic from concentrating on accumulating practical assets. In general, the 7 will not be escapists. However, this number's negative aspects indicate teasing, melancholy, and dismay when finances go badly, and relationships tax their emotions. Unfortunately, these introspective talents are not likely to discuss their emotional issues. They may seem sloppy or disconnected, but they actually feel everything in depth. The 7 finds it difficult to trust others, so they seek information within themselves. When balanced, whoever has self-expression number 7 knows when to act based on careful consideration.

Destiny

The insightful and perceptive nature of 7s enables them to work well in professions that require deep insight and understanding into others' feelings and the structures of the world. Also, 7s will gravitate toward creative professions in which great courage is needed to innovate. Suggested Occupations: Psychiatrist, psychologist, psychotherapist, scientist, specialist technician, engineer, computer programmer, systems analyst, mathematician, editor, judge, photographer, underwater explorer, oceanographer, geologist, historian, etc.

Personal Year

The number 7 is the seventh of the nine-year cycle of experiences that results in the agility and performance qualification based on the goals set in the first year. It is time to rest, reflect, and analyze. Let go of the domestic and emotional sacrifice of the previous year. March usher in an age of personal values, non-commercial approaches, and self-analysis as the spring and summer months do not lead to commercial ambitions or physical overload.

For most, it's a slow year, filled with delays in communication, legal issues, and unexpected feelings of loneliness. For the others, the year focuses on a path of specialized studies that was decided to take place in October of the previous year. And introspective year, convenient to the examination of the past and the planning of the future. Money and practical achievements will appear as long as the individual is not very mutant or aggressive.

Do not be afraid to pass business or material interests to the background. Recognize this experience, unique in nine years, to see life, choose priorities, and learn from the past. Do not move. Keep calm. Do not rush the stations or handle the days. The most promising plans will work under control, or you let in things that might be beneficial. If aggressive attitudes are taken, the financial and material activities to come will be delayed. Problems arise that force you to think about why you have been feeling helpless or repressed. A serene attitude is beneficial. It is not important whether you understand how things will happen for the better: it is important to hope for the best, have faith, and take rest from external responsibilities and ambitions. This year aims to remind you that life is not just what you see.

Personal year number 7 encourages the development of new interests and deeper understandings. The ideas generate investigations that materialize in the commercial achievements of the following year. In order to gain mobility and freedom to pursue commercial or material ambitions the following year, health is a factor to be considered now. Medical and dental reviews should be planned before July as preventive measures. Any physical malaise must be identified and immediately referred to a professional. If the intellectual, spiritual, or physical preparations are ignored, it is because the year is not being used wisely. Intuitive decisions that have been made and archived for future use will determine the scope of maturity harvested in the last six months.

Personal Month

Personal month number 7 in any one year provides the opportunity to question the plans, enlist the help of professionals and learn from the past. Attitudes should be taken only the following month. Wait, and you will see that the answers you will have are appropriate for legal negotiations, questionable alliances, and current progressive ideas. A broad, curious, and demanding point of view must have absolute priority. Aggressiveness, commercial ambitions, and unnecessary social interactions must be put aside. Remember to say, "I'll think." Examine others' opinions carefully and think before you speak. Do not reveal your thoughts; be a little secretive. This is not a good time to get a phone call. When the phone rings, you will receive data. Take time to read, self-test, and savor philosophical discussions. Be patient, tolerant, and feel like spending time in silence. This can be an exceptionally illuminated month.

Personal Day

Wake up with a leisure attitude, do not overload the physical, and avoid confusion or conflict. Address each experience with calm, serenity, and posture.

Whatever the task, focus on preparation and accuracy. Review to get the most out of a situation. Be receptive and listen to the ideas of others. It is a day of lingering long in personal plans, character traits, and the non-material side of expectations. Commercial delays or technical issues will overwhelm, solutions will not be readily available, and arrangements for solving problems must be made only tomorrow.

Today, other people are likely to postpone making commitments or living up to their promises. An expected phone call or letter may not arrive. But the moon will continue to rise, and the sun will set as usual, despite the stumbling of the day. It is best to remain passive and not be disturbed by what happens. If possible, continue reading informative books, go to the movies or let the imagination roam freely when listening to music. The practical problems will solve themselves. Make a personal commitment to improving yourself. Be honest and reflect on past behavior to see how to change or eliminate unproductive habits. Take some time to look happier and healthier. Your abstract thoughts can become practical accomplishments if you are inspired and have faith. Take care of medical or dental obligations. Talk to a psychologist, lawyer, or accountant if you need professional knowledge. Gain knowledge and advise to others—without thinking of compensation. Tomorrow's concentration on efficiency, life force, and material goals will bring the opportunity for tangible results.

Chapter 12: Number 8 – Material Power

Attributes

Positive – Efficient, Reliable, Strong, Self-Ambitious, Discerning, Insightful, Functional, Affirmative, Intelligent.

Negative – Materialist, Intolerant, Tired, Dishonest, Disheartened, Undisciplined, Thirsty for Power, Sullen, Coarse

Correspondents

LETTERS: H, Z

NUMBERS: 26, 35, 44, 53, 62, 71, 80, 89, 98, 107

COLOR: Pink, Reddish-Pink, Mauve

GEM: Diamond

CRYSTAL: Pyrite, Morganite Pink Beryl Rosy

VEGETATION: Begonia, Dahlia, Jasmine, Nogueira Pine Tree, Rhododendron

FOODS: Cereals, Bacon, Rice, Cauliflower, Chicken, Tea, Apple Pie

INSTRUMENTS/MUSICAL APPEAL: Hawaiian Guitar, Coral, Soprano, Theatre of Magazine

MUSICAL NOTE: Acute

PLANET: Saturn

MONTH: August

DATEDAYS OF BIRTH: 8, 17, 26

DAY OF THE WEEK: Thursday

GENERAL COMPATIBILITY NUMBERS: 2, 4, 6

INCOMPATIBILITY NUMBERS: 7, 8, 9

Note: When the individual bears the challenge of number 8, these descriptions are no longer positive to negative until the challenge is balanced. Please be sure to read the meaning of the number of the code.

Challenges of the Number 8

This is the challenge to the individual's understanding of the values and purposes of money and power. As children, the bearers of this challenge may have seen authorities with unreasonable ambitions that focused on the financial picture. Power at a high level and competitive spirit were the only means available to achieve freedom—or the opposite extreme may have been tried, and in this case, the authorities may have had no interest in accumulating assets, in influencing the competitiveness. Either of these extremes gave young people 8 false sense of material values and fostered a greater or lesser obsession with material possessions and financial security. Consequently, the individual bearers of the challenge usually become self-employed or self-destructive, without a goal. As adolescents, individuals with this challenge may excel in sports, school work, or part-time employment after school hours. They may be considered super-young or, at the opposite extreme, these adolescents may become unreasonable, incoherent, and unrelated. They may be unable to make good judgments, order their affairs, or take responsibility for managing time, money, and practical obligations. For those with this challenge, the concern with self-control is either too much, or insufficient. Or they are gales, or breezes, with temperaments compatible with each end.

These individuals may think, "Who will reject me if I have money, power, and prestige?" However, responses tell them that people cannot be treated as if they are business structures. Certain 8s should learn that there is a power superior to the board. To master the challenge of 8, one must first master the challenge of number 7, who has faith in non-material values and recognizes the wisdom in every man.

Challenge number 8 can move from one to the other of the following extremes until it is recognized and begin new habits that stabilize the material ambitions of its bearer.

- Very combative or very apathetic.
- Very unruly or very ethical.

- Very aggressive or very slow.
- Very ambitious or very chaotic.
- Very efficient or very incompetent.
- Too defensive or too defenseless.
- Very controllable or very unreliable.
- Very limited or very expansive.
- Very sloppy or very upright.
- Too forgetful or too conscious.
- Very busy or very lazy.
- Very dynamic or very fragile.
- Very wasteful or very economical.
- Very exhibitionist or very careless.

Physical Challenges of the Number 8

This list of diseases and negative habits is related to the challenge of number 8.

- Addictions
- Herpes
- Alcoholism
- Indigestion
- Allergy
- Clutches at the joints
- Appendicitis
- Laryngeal Asthma
- Nervousness

- Cold
- Skin Problems
- Eczema
- Disk
- Herniation Epilepsy
- Smoking Problems
- Eye Problems
- Fainting Spells
- Varicose Veins
- Heart Problems
- Warts
- Hepatitis

Balancing the Challenges of the Number 8

The first step in balancing the challenge is to feel free to say, "I need material freedom." Take a look at personal relationships. Do not forget to thank the secretary for the consideration shown outside the job specifications. Invite a friend over for a formal lunch. Set a goal to organize your time to include a hobby, a nimble walk, or a quiet night with loved ones. Force yourself to read books that speak of the lives of billionaires and ask yourself if money actually bought them all.

Keep in mind that you find the same people you encountered on the climb as descending. Be generous, considerate, and respect people for what they do. It is impossible to accomplish anything in a world full of caciques. Every cacique needs loyal Indians to take care of the details, so protect your tribe and make it happy.

Automotive

Youth:

As a child, the number 8 feels a tremendous drive to be attentive, self-reliant, and active. When rebuked, this child can avail himself of a well-kept treasure, stare confidently, and exchange tricks to relieve his wounded ego. This child needs exercises, practical tasks, and interactions with peers, as the young number 8 is generally courageous, managerial, and decisive. When surrounded by weak or unreasonable authorities, crack the whip. You want discipline, and you figure out how to do it.

Children number 8 need to plan, build, and work consistently. His cleverness, ability to concentrate, and intellectual curiosity must be coordinated with physical activities. Lack of interest in artistic self-expression or the difficulty in accepting the vulnerability of others can be a problem in maturity. The 8 are born organizers and fall to convince everyone to help them. By virtue of his ability to see the intimacy of unrealistic people and his outspoken criticism, his parents, if they wish to avoid disrespectful confrontations, must practice what they teach or find out that their children are directing them.

Maturity:

The number 8 adults want to own and enjoy all that money can buy. They strive to be influential and lead a well-organized and constructive lifestyle, preferring traditional marriage and creating a family that shares their ambitions. However, these 8 are the self-mediators who have no respect for weakness, procrastination, or failure. They may, therefore, have no eyes for the partner's emotional anxieties or for the concepts of relaxed holidays or non-organizational social activities. People number 8 do not like to be disobeyed, disorganized, or distracted by small details. Since they are seldom content to pay the bills, they prefer to gravitate to the big businessmen. The 8 must have the latest Gucci wallet, the latest Mercedes-Benz model, or some other prestige accessory. These individuals can swim 20 laps in a pool, lift weights or run 20 kilometers before or after work. They have formidable vitality and physical stamina, and therefore need leaks to relieve stress—which they seem to nurture. Rest or relax, on the other hand, annoys you.

Balanced 8 will take success seriously. Nervous schemes and sloppy work habits indicate fear of failure and the underlying inability to self-govern. The Balanced 8 believes that it takes money to make money, and his approach to finances is realistic and conscientious. However, this perception does not compensate for its possible blindness concerning the intimate ones that offer him love and consolation.

Self-Image

Youth:

When lying in bed, listening to music and thinking, "How will I grow up? How will I walk, dress and talk?" the 8-year-old pre-teens envision an industrial giant, the host of the major sports, an immortal sportsman. They dream of being CEOs at some board, going out after lunch for a business talk on the company's yacht, receiving the Sportsman of the Year trophy, or training to death a winning team. Children with the self-image number 8 look rich and, above all, winners—CEOs, professional athletes, and financial advisors.

Maturity:

When they leave the elevator or enter a room—before the personality or intellect comes into action—the number 8 adults emit a marked, benign, and impertinent vibration. His attitude indicates a strong personality and seems to exude energy. The first impression they make is thriving, domineering, and dignified. When the meanings of numbers of self-motivation and self-expression are artistic or modest, they display the symbols of prestige, and their dress style, posture, and attitude signal to the world that they do not cost cheap.

Self-Expression

Youth:

The number 8 talents lead the child to work early. They will be more competent, consistent, and more effective adults if they are encouraged to manage finances, time, and energy properly. To reach the ambitious goals they draw for themselves, they need affirmation, workmanship, and life force. However, once they have the opportunity to solve their practical problems on their own, the number 8 children demonstrate that they trust in themselves.

As a teenager and young adult, the 8 are always busy and must learn to relax, have good school grades, play on the varsity, become a class president, and make money after school. They have a talent for big business. These young people are serious finance students and have the knack for getting a return on their physical and commercial efforts.

Maturity:

When 8s are able to become centered in their chosen profession, they age well into it. They tend to become industry experts and innovators. They can find ways of improving processes and finding dimensions to their chosen areas that others may not have been able to find. 8s tend to have success later on in their career since all those years of cumulative study and reflection lead them to attain a degree of mastery that very few are able to achieve.

8s have the potential to be rewarded financially for their executive ability, their efficiency, and their commercial practice. It is possible to be recognized for its vital force and physical coordination. The 8 are domineering personalities who plan, organize, and work to make the most of their efforts. These individuals emit vibrations that puts them in the driver's armchair.

Number 8's must recognize their need to maintain a positive approach. In a business or sports environment, they are reservoirs of solutions to problems that radiate force. When asked to socialize and promote, the 8 have the skills to delight and impress the most prestigious clients. They are persuasive opportunists when they know what they want—and usually, know it. And it is possible to count that the balanced number 8 will be employees and conscious employers. They demonstrate impertinent style and position in their attire and enjoy displaying an air of prosperity, power, and ability.

Destiny:

The high degree of conscientiousness of 8s leads them to excel in jobs that require tenacity and resiliency. They are also geared toward occupations that require a profound study of the subject matter at hand. Here are some of the best occupations for 8s: manufacturer, banker, stockbroker, financial adviser, professional sportsman, military officer, statistician, accountant, office manager, engineer, band conductor, drummer, business lawyer, construction contractor, construction supervisor, payroll administrator, investor, cashier, controller, bank loan manager, franchise operator, collection manager, civil servant, union leader, sales manager, farmer, importer/exporter, weight lifter, physical fitness consultant, film producer, and director of theatrical production.

Personal Year

The number 8 is the eighth in the nine-year cycle of experiences that result in the predictability and performance qualification based on the goals set in the first year. In February, the individual sows ideas that spring up in April. During the first and last weeks of September, activity intensifies, money is collected, and influential alliances. For most, finances improve, and new opportunities result from projects postponed and reviewed in the previous year.

It is the year in which you see the tangible results of past efforts. If romance is the goal, the prospects for wealth, health, and ambition are more easily realized.

Single-sex flirts can uncover sparks of sexual activity in June. If marriage is the goal, it's time to hone your nerves to go out in search of a meaningful relationship. A business approach is both dating and taking control of a company. You need to ignore the petty problems and use the ability to plan and manage effectively to achieve the goals at work. It's time to go after what you want in the hope of getting it.

Personal Month

Personal month number 8, in any personal year, provides the opportunity to take control of commercial and financial affairs. You must always rely on yourself, be energetic and resourceful. Powerful, entrepreneurial, and pragmatic acquaintances are important now. It's not the time to take a holiday, sensitize, or take unruly behavior. After delays, legal problems, and unanswered questions from the previous month, you need to develop an efficient attitude and break the wheels of progress. The projects started seven months ago require the maximum effort: to advertise, promote, and be insightful. One must dress with dignity, be diplomatic, and display all the prestige symbols available. When it is organized and persuasive, the results achieved will be exceptional.

Personal Day

Wake up to the goals in mind and propose to fulfill them. Sketch plans and expect to fulfill them. Check the expenses, be careful, and try to see far, making the day is profitable and orderly. There will be money coming in or going out on account of the bargains. Shopping, marketing ideas, and socializing for business are the favorite activities. Look successful: remember, money attracts money, and the dominant impressions attract the domain.

On-time, ask for a raise, an office with a panoramic view, or plan to travel first class. Be direct, expect to achieve results, and everything will run smoothly. Do not be ungainly, obstinate, or self-indulgent. Keep your appearance dignified and affirmative and boost self-confidence. Fragile attempts, fear of failure, and offensive rhetoric emit cowardly vibrations. Be brave and expect to be respected. Otherwise, this day's very strong energy will internalize itself in the form of restrictions and frustration.

"Invest" in bookmarks if there are late payments. Today, you are more likely to receive debts or favors. Do not take risks, do not lose your temper, and do not be foolish. In strange situations, be the first to maintain refinement, confidence, and conscious leadership. Remember that whoever is in power is watching. Today's energetic, enthusiastic, and forward executive efforts can bring material rewards tomorrow. Success depends on common sense, logic, and problem solving constructively. If you keep the goals in mind, it will be a memorable day.

Chapter 13: Number 9 And 0 – Conclusions

Attributes

Positive – Compassion, Empathy, Art, Faith, Generosity, Compatibility, Bravery, Tenderness, Voluntariness, Tolerance.

Negative – Bitterness, Fanaticism, Selfishness, Jealousy, Indiscrimination, Inconstancy, Coldness, Disappointment, Covetousness

Correspondents

LETTERS: I, R

NUMBERS: 18, 27, 36, 45, 54, 63, 72, 81, 90, 99, 108

COLOR: Saffron, Orange-Yellow-Gold

GEMS: Opal

CRYSTALS: Alunite

VEGETATION: Holly, Magnolia, Gold Bud, Oak, Banana

FOOD: Milk, Cheese, Beef Boi, Jelly

INSTRUMENTS/MUSICAL APPEAL: Violin, Tenor, Symphony

MUSICAL NOTE: Acute

PLANET: Mars

MONTH: September

DAYS OF BIRTH: 9, 18, 27

DAY OF THE WEEK: Tuesday

NUMBERS OF GENERAL COMPATIBILITY: 5, 6, 9,1 (Artistic); 3, 8 (Business)

INCOMPATIBILITY NUMBERS: 4, 7

Note: When the individual has the challenge of number 9, these descriptions will go from positive to negative until the challenge is balanced. Please be sure to read the meaning of the challenge number.

The Challenges of the Numbers 9 and 0

This is the challenge to the individual understanding of human emotions and fragility. The bearer of this challenge is born with the maturity of an "old soul," which is philosophical and has more opportunities than the average person. So you have immediate personal choice. It has the ability to know what is wrong, how to repair it, and also great potential for compassion, empathy, and solving beneficent problems.

In youth, adults may have expected too much from these young people, even more than they can understand or achieve. Generally speaking, these children are born to parents who have passed the average age of having children. In some cases, they are the middle children of large families, who run the tightrope because they have to obey the older, domineering brothers and father the younger brothers. A serious illness can have them hospitalized or left under the care of adults at home. These children were asked to understand serious personal problems or the emotional ups and downs of younger or older relatives who surrounded them.

When pre-teens and teens, they are loners. They can go from class to class in the pursuit of their performance models or exemplary people of an art or craft. They fall in love at a distance, have difficulty with intimate relationships, and often fall in love with passion. The 9 or 0 have so much to give that they cannot give it just to one person, or else they sink into the needs of their lovers.

Young people, number 9 can take on responsibilities, become group leaders, and nullify themselves for their peers' welfare. As adults, they continue to give more than they receive or else face the world with selfishness. The 9, unconsciously, feel deprived of youth's dreamed joys and try to stay young forever. They usually marry older or more educated individuals or young people, and the neediest individuals. Either they serve the community or live at the state's expense; they are freshmen or "old souls."

Challenge 0 can swing from one to the other of the following extremes until you are identified and begin new habits that impersonate your carrier's emotions and entice you to make choices and changes.

- Very deprived or very selfish.
- Very airy mentally or very fanatical.
- Very melodramatic or very unimpressive.
- Very satisfied or very unhappy.
- Very possessive or very liberal.
- Very dispassionate or very romantic.
- Very understanding or very hard.
- Very charitable or very greedy.
- Very brave or very cowardly.
- Very fickle or very loyal.
- Very provincial or very cultured.

- Very stubborn or very receptive.
- Very dedicated or very careless.
- Very vindictive or very forgiving.

Physical Challenges of the Numbers 9 and 0

This list of illnesses and negative habits relates to the development of Number 9 and 0.

- Problems in the Back
- Swollen Bone
- Jealousy Problems
- Bronchitis
- Problems in the Knees
- Cellulite Problems
- Lung Problems
- Problems in the Eyes
- Pneumonia
- Glandular Problems
- Sea Gout
- Problems in the Breasts
- Headaches
- Stuttering
- Cardiac arrest
- Venereal disease

- Warts

Balancing the Challenges of the Numbers 9 and 0

The first step in balancing the challenge is to feel free to say, "I need to be needed." Select priorities, and remember that you have a good reason to follow your feelings. Resolve your ambitions now. Be decisive, and you will receive positive responses. You have the ability to see all the options. Analyze your priorities: find an advantageous angle from which you can cultivate your compassion, solidarity, and desire to rise.

Open your heart to counter the urge to be possessive. You cannot be tied to purely domestic or community needs. You have the ability to set the example to be followed by others. But do not feel needy if your students might become your teachers. This is a great honor, and the greater credit will be yours.

Automotive

Youth:

As a child, the impulse that Number 9 feels is to be affectionate, empathetic, and jealous of your circumstances. When rebuked, this child understands the feelings of authority, becomes emotional and apologizes, or throws all the blame on the accuser. This child needs love, from sensitive social interactions, and from the sense of being needed. The young number 9 is kind, caring, and well-meaning. When surrounded by distanced authorities, he remains impassive or willful. He wants heat and goes to extremes to get it.

The 9 want to be multitalented communicators. They should explore interests in music, arts, sports, theatre, and writing. When the medium leads to spiritual or religious observation, children 9 offer an answer. However, they can transfer from one faith system to another that accumulates knowledge. The 9 tend to disseminate their interests, their beneficent efforts, and their romantic ideas. They may dream for a time that they were born to be saints. When they know that the saints have to live the hell on earth to be considered, they decide to play Helen Hayes or Richard Burton, becoming worshiped stars of the theatre.

Maturity:

The number 9 adults want to live a worthwhile life. They will find it difficult to narrow their interests and concentrate on mundane practices or immediate needs. The 9s are led to help others and create or engage with universal artistic merit. They have inspired sanitarians and altruistic reformers who want to benefit the world. They are capable of self-sacrifice even when they have little and practice great deeds for petty people. The 9 want security, but they do little to stabilize their economy, emotions, or movements.

People number 9 do not like being tied to the house or having their emotions suppressed. Almost always unable to confine themselves to a single intimate relationship, they have many groups of friends. The 9 should go where they are needed. A less fortunate stranger, a loss-making charity, or a theatrical company looking for actresses or audiences touches their hearts or their pockets. These individuals practice generous, sentimental, and impulsive gestures. They feel the pain of the other with a sense of immediacy difficult to be tolerated in every day for the most intimate.

Self-Image

Youth:

Lying in bed, listening to music, and thinking, "How am I going to be when I grow up? How am I going to walk, dress, and talk?" Pre-adolescent number 9 sees himself as a wise counselor, a dedicated artist, or a stripped-down humanitarian, dreams of receiving the Nobel Peace Prize and donate the money to a charity.

Self-images number 9 relate to pleasing others. They make promises and try to keep them. The first impression the 9 people make is romantic, artistic, and strong. And your youthful desire possesses the emotional and physical ability to take on everyone's problems and relieve the universal signs of suffering. At times they may seem overly dramatic. When they feel attuned to self-image, they subjugate their personalities and material ambitions to stimulate a lover or collaborate for a cause they respect.

Maturity:

When they leave the elevator or enter a room—before the personality or intellect takes action—the number 9 adults emit friendly vibrations. Often graying early, the 9 seem wise and dignified—never old and broken. His attitude indicates a gracious personality and seems to exude the aura of well-intentioned interest. The first impression they make is magnetic.

When they use the saffron color—a yellow-orange mixture reminiscent of autumn leaves—the self-image is enhanced. The self-image individual number 9 need not convince or strive to persuade others to be equal to himself. In essence, 9 includes the talents of communication of the number 3, the talents of representation and communication and the communitarian services of the number 6, and the talents of teaching and communication of the theatre of the airy number 9. The first impression that causes an emotionally stimulated number 9 can be intense and passionately lively. And an expert in feeling the needs of others and playing the expected role. This impressionable idealist has the temperament of a great goddess or an eccentric artist.

The 9 are born leaders. Without experience or preparation, they join the groups and set the example that others choose to follow. When they live according to their self-image, they are affectionate, hospitable, and tolerant.

Self-Expression

Youth:

Without the intention of exaggerating, the compassionate number 9 may, in a heroic gesture, return to a burning building to save a pet or relative. The 9 think about the well-being of others, examine the general picture, and practice deprived acts. They imitate adults and copy colleagues. The 9 are funny, free-form, and fanciful. They inspire confidence and are extremely intuitive. Materialistic, possessive, narrow-minded parents may seem too emotional, generous, or expansive. For educated, artistic, and broad-minded adults, the number 9 children are students and teachers who need to be enlightened at every opportunity.

Teenagers number 9 and young adults are forthright, discerning, and attractive. They have many friends and various interests that keep them away from home. These teens have distant correspondents, spend time with the old and infirm, and play Hamlet or Ophelia at the Shakespearean school festival. They are adept at words, and writing, interpreting, and talking are easy things. These children of universal love are intimidated by commercial ambitions, exclusiveness, and pessimism. They are willing to save or serve the world and need to work in a job that offers extensive benefits.

Maturity:

Individuals number 9 have the potential to financially reward themselves with the ability to communicate their understanding of human nature. They are artists of unique talent, expert interpreters who realize their abilities and establish examples worthy of note. It is possible by the recognition of their ability to empathize with people to respond to the needs of others and to delight and win great audiences. The basic attributes of number 9 are the taste for the world, the nobility of purpose, and dispossession. These individuals emit a vibration that puts them at the receiving end of the problems of others. The number 9 talents should recognize your need to inspire, teach, and overestimate others. They have a great capacity for impersonal love and charity. The business environment, the competitiveness of colleagues, and the commercial aggressiveness make us nervous and stun your creativity. The 9 are excellent in the areas of development and counseling. Sales and marketing may or may not attract them. If your profession requires diversification of attitudes, you will have the ability to make a simple sale or a solemn promotion at an informal meeting. As lecturers, they are excellent, along with a wide variety of audiences. It can be said that balanced 9 are open, airy, and trustworthy. They are usually artistic, charming, and neat—predicates in the organization of services or communication.

Destiny

Number 9s enjoy communicating and relating to others. They are apt to help others develop their own talents. They are also keen on improving themselves and the world. Here are some suggested occupations: Editor, writer, reporter, foreign correspondent, editor in chief, circulation manager, teacher, teacher assistant, physician, lecturer, artist, illustrator, social worker, welfare administrator, university administrator, preacher, etc.

Personal Year

The number 9 is the new year in the nine-cycle of experiences that results in the agility and performance qualification based on the goals set in the first year. In the spring, the individual receives recognition of creative efforts, takes inventory of past accomplishments, and prepares to begin new long-term goals. For the most part, old boyfriends, college mates, and personal ideals spring up and are the subject of definitive evaluation. In addition, a year to discard the clothes that went out of style, re-read the favorite books, and abandon lost loves. It is time for reflection and reassessment. This year requires unconditional love and acceptance of the problems of others. Nothing new begins, so anything that insinuates a fresh start the next year should be eliminated.

Changes are necessary, so certain things must be completed. The new targets instigated in October disappear by the end of the year and should be kept until April of the following year. Transitions emerge that germinate in October. You have to select your priorities. You can plan in the fall, but it's best not to instigate innovative change, but with all the facts at hand. Time should be spent to improve relationships, entertain, counsel, or inspire others.

Personal Month

The personal month in any one-year period provides the opportunity to complete projects, be charitable, and expand cultural activities. Personal ambitions will not be favored, nor will commercial aggression. Instead, it's time to inspire, counsel, and support others. Projects that started eight months ago flourish and will be completed or abandoned. Situations that require altruism and open-mindedness arise. Visit the sick, the elderly, or the needy, bringing them a book, a tasty treat, or a good ear. This is not the time to start anything! Group interactions, auditions, and public appearances enhance your reputation and attract rewards. Use this month to find outstanding or helpful people who have contacts or the ability to foster ambitions.

Personal Day

Wake up with a pleasant word and determination to solve all problems before sunset. Pass by the house of a friend in need and do something caring for him. Plan to share blessings, talents, and understanding. Use the day to tell the fanatic on the other street to grow up, and make sure that personal bias is not transparent. Detailed work may require effort too. It's best to put off the sewing, the iron, and the conversations with the accountant for a few days. It is a day to think about important issues and be generous with lovers, friends, and co-workers.

You will notice that there are giblets that need to be clarified and resolved. And the impulse to consolidate and to get out of the way everything that has been dragging is great. Make a personal commitment to be patient, forgiving, and well-meaning. Do not mix things up. Divide knowledge and let people who have lived and assimilated more than you enlighten them.

You will focus on people in cultural expansion and forgiving experiences. Listen to music, watch a play, or volunteer to donate blood. The only thing you can give that saves lives and restores itself in six hours is blood. Remember, to be creative, you first need to admire the art of others. It's time to get deep satisfaction by relating to your fellow humans and the universe.

Accept everything that happens today and is pleasant. Realize that there is an hour when it is necessary to give demonstrations of compassion, consideration, and tolerance. Certain sacrifices may be necessary. On this day, you may be blamed for someone else's mistake, or you can forgive and forget a slip. This day should be used to reflect, expand, or complete, and plan tomorrow's changes.

Above all, use the time to tie loose ends and not expect anything new to start.

Conclusion

Thank you for making it through to the end of Numerology: Decoding Your Destiny, let's hope it was informative and able to provide you with all of the tools you need to achieve your goals in life.

By gaining a deeper understanding of Numerology, you begin to understand the inner workings of your personality and the people around you. This makes life easier to navigate and gives you the power to work with what you have to succeed in all facets of life.

This type of knowledge and insight is certainly able to make you much more sensitive to what drives you and your personal needs. More importantly, it can also help you be in tune with the needs of others around you. As a result, you will be able to better communicate your needs and wants while connecting with others on a much deeper and meaningful level.

Please go refer back to this book as often as you need in order to clear up any questions you may have about the specifics of each number. Moreover, do keep this book handy since you will find yourself "reading" people all the time. As you gain more proficiency with each of the numbers in this book, you will develop a keen sense of the types of personalities people around your display.

If you have found this book useful and informative, do tell your friends, family, colleagues, and anyone who might be interested in this topic about it. They will surely find it to be as interesting as you have.

www.ingramcontent.com/pod-product-compliance
Lightning Source LLC
Chambersburg PA
CBHW081344070526
44578CB00005B/715